WHAT YOU NEED TO KNOW

using **email** effectively

using
email
effectively

LINDA LAMB & JERRY PEEK

O'REILLY & ASSOCIATES, INC.
103 Morris Street, Suite A
Sebastopol, CA 95472

Using Email Effectively
Linda Lamb and Jerry Peek

Editor: Linda Lamb

Production Editors: Ellen Siever and Stephen Spainhour

Printing History:

      April 1995   First Edition

ISBN: 1-56592-103-8   [6/95]

Table of Contents

CHAPTER 1

What you need to know before you do anything else　　1

> You can learn the rock-bottom basics of email by asking for a tutorial at your
> office. We point you to places where you can get help with your mailer's com-
> mands. We explain message lists and the concept of the current message, as
> well as the commands for reading, printing, deleting, and saving messages.

CHAPTER 2

What you need to know to communicate well　　19

> Some practices irritate email readers—messages that are unnecessarily long
> or confusing, or negotiations that should be conducted by another communi-
> cation method. We look at when to use the phone instead of email; ways that
> a "private" email message can become public; how to include past messages;
> tried-and-true rules for using capitals, tabs, line length, white space, etc. And
> we give you hints for seeing your mail through others' eyes.

CHAPTER 3

What you need to know to be productive 33

Productivity depends on what you use email for, as well as on some tricks of the trade. We invite you to look at how you're using email. Then we describe productivity hints such as the "sort" and "pick" commands; acting on a group of messages; reading a file into your message; using company-wide and personal aliases.

CHAPTER 4

What you need to know to organize saved mail 49

There is no one "right" way to organize saved mail; the "right" way depends on the person doing the saving. We talk about using the inbox for active messages and using other folders (or mailboxes) for saved messages; organizing and naming folders; listing folders; moving to folders; removing old folders.

CHAPTER 5

What you need to know to send mail over networks 59

Email is very reliable so long as the address is correct. We look at the variety of addressing styles; the two parts of an address (the who and the where); how to tell if an address looks right; how to translate addresses from one network style to another; some simple troubleshooting; and the cost of receiving messages over the network.

CHAPTER 6

What you need to know about mailing lists 75

Mailing lists are group discussions. Subscribing and unsubscribing to lists are often shrouded in mystery, because people do this so infrequently. We examine mailing list subjects; administration; the two addresses you should know for every list; how to subscribe and unsubscribe from a list; posting to a list; the finer points such as setting digests and acknowledgments.

CHAPTER 7

What you need to know to customize your environment 89

Mailers let you set variables, either through menu options or in a set-up file. We describe creating a signature file; automatically saving outgoing mail; modifying how your mailer alerts you to new mail; changing the information in the list of headers; printing messages; reading mail remotely; creating your own comands.

What you need to know about this book

Shorten your learning curve.

Using Email Effectively is aimed at anyone who uses a PC or UNIX mailer. Most of you probably already know, or are learning, the basics of sending mail (what buttons to push).

If you've read email, you know that some messages are irritating or get ignored. Other messages communicate clearly and appropriately; their senders get listened to.

How do you become one of those senders who sends mail that gets read? How can you learn the ropes of editing an included message, finding old messages, subscribing to a mailing list, or corresponding with people on other networks? How do you get the larger context that lets you make the best use of this necessary business tool? The answer is usually experience. Experience plus being very observant and having a few expert users you can ask questions of.

We hope that this book helps you to sound smarter, sooner. We believe that even most "old hands" at email will discover some new parts of the bigger picture—pointers about network addressing, mailing lists, or sending files.

The "right way" to use email varies by circumstance.

When Jerry Peek and I began work on the material for this book, I suspected that there was probably a "right" way to use email—and it wasn't mine. Surely the "right" way to use email must be more technically adept than my own and vastly more organized. I hoped to find this "right" method by interviewing others. But while I was interviewing, I kept running into conflicts:

- Tim (O'Reilly) is adamant about ignoring email long enough to set his own priorities; Frank (Willison) finds it valuable to be blown off course by email.

- Arsenio (Santos) continually clears his queue of email, answering the oldest messages first; Allen (Noren) keeps messages in the queue until the queue reaches 600 and then deletes the first 200 messages in one fell swoop.

- Edie (Freedman) has an organization for saved mail that is so clear, an outsider to her job could find any message; Hugh (Brown) saves few messages, except those he prints out to take with him on the road.

What I found was that the email "ideal" depends on the person using it. It depends on a lot of specifics: How many messages do you get in a day? What kinds of communication does your organization use email for? Are you subscribed to mailing lists? Are you online all day or just sporadically? What email programs and support are available at your site? How many of your clients, coworkers, colleagues, and friends have email?

So, although we'll make plenty of suggestions, you'll find your own "right" way.

This series puts technology in context.

Like other books we've published, the "What You Need to Know" series started with a need that we had for a certain kind of information. Tim (O'Reilly) noticed that we had nothing to give our own nontechnical employees about subjects they needed to understand in order to work here productively. The kind of information our users need is not "Push this button." It's more "Here's how to think about this."

After someone has been working in our office for a while, she learns that she shouldn't send an "I'll be out this afternoon" message to 70 people. She knows not to use a one-size-fits-all mail alias, but instead to think about who will be getting her message and whether they need to see it. But there isn't an easy way for people to get that kind of general knowledge except through painful experience (their's and everyone else's).

So we developed a series of books to tackle the issues encountered by people like many of us at O'Reilly & Associates (ORA)—people who use technology as a tool for their "real" job. These books digest and present the kind of information you'd come across if you worked with the technology for a while, in a supportive and knowledgeable environment. These are books we will be handing to our own employees.

This book is designed to be browsable.

Depending on how you want to read the book, you can get your information from first-person stories, frequent headlines that tell the gist of each short section, the text itself, or reference sections. We have sidebars of users telling stories, because people learn from personal experiences. (After you've seen someone embarrass themselves company-wide by misaddressing their mail, you'll be sure to check the To: field in your own messages.) So, we have users telling about their embarrassing moments and their personal ways of looking at technology. The anecdotes aren't fluff to cajole you through the material. They ARE what you need to know. By reading the stories alone, you can get the gist of the material in the chapter.

Headings that summarize main points and short, stand-alone sections also encourage browsing. How-to sections are distinguished by their own format, so that you can easily skip—or find—specific procedures.

Of course, reading straight through all the chapters is also an option. We hope that when you "dip in," you'll find so much of use that you'll keep reading.

You can contact us to suggest improvements or to buy in bulk.

Please write to us if you have suggestions for improving this book (or even to relate a favorite email story). You can find us at:

O'Reilly & Associates, Inc.
103 A Morris Street
Sebastopol CA 95472
707-829-0515, Fax 829-0104

By email: *info@ora.com* **(via the Internet)** or *uunet!ora!info* **(via UUCP)**

To ask technical questions or comment on the book, send email to:

   bookquestions@ora.com

For information on volume discounts for bulk purchase, call O'Reilly & Associates, Inc. at 800-998-9938 or send email to *linda@ora.com* (*uunet!ora.com!linda*). For companies requiring extensive customization of the book, some licensing terms are also available.

We'd like to thank others.

Jerry Peek and I both worked on this book. Jerry, who is an expert on MH, xmh, and other UNIX mailers, wrote the entire first draft of this book in about a week and a half on his laptop in the great outdoors. I spent many months defining ideas for the series and then changing the draft to match the defined audience and the tone of the series.

We'd like to thank all those who agreed to be interviewed and included in this book: Jane Appleyard, Olivia Bogdan, Liz Bradley, Hugh Brown, Mary Jane Caswell-Stephenson, Stephanie Davis, Edie Freedman, Glenn Harden, John Labovitz, Allen Noren, Ted Meister, Linda Mui, Tim O'Reilly, Ron Petrusha, Arsenio Santos, Linda Walsh, Larry Watson, and Frank Willison.

We'd like to thank those who agreed to have their signature files included in this book: Chris Casey, Rosemary Dean Mackintosh, Cynthia Pribram, Peter Schmitt, Paul Schwartz, Scott Senften, and Tony Thomas.

Thanks to John Labovitz and Glenn Harden, who talked with me about sending files; Arsenio Santos, who helped a number of times when I was technically stuck; and Ron Petrusha, for helping me to partially overcome a command-line mailer bias.

Thanks to the production and design departments of O'Reilly & Associates, especially Ellen Siever for her thorough copyediting, Stephen Spainhour for getting the book through production, Mike Sierra for his FrameMaker magic, Donna Woonteiler and Seth Maislin for indexing, Jennifer Niederst for her beautiful book design, Leslie Evans for her portrait illustrations, and also Sheryl Avruch, Kismet McDonough, and portrait scanner extraordinaire, Nancy Priest.

I'd like to thank Tim O'Reilly for giving me the chance and encouragement to do some things that I love. I'd also like to thank Tim and the other people at O'Reilly who have put so much of themselves into this company, especially Linda Walsh and Cathy Brennan. It's been a wonderful place to be for the past ten years.

I'd like to dedicate my efforts on this book to my children, Olivia Bogdan and Jack Bogdan.

CHAPTER I

What you need to know before you do anything else

First, ask your coworkers a few questions.

This chapter describes the basic actions you can take with any mail program, but it's no substitute for a hands-on tutorial on your mailer. If someone in your office has not already explained the basics of your email program, ask for 20 minutes of time. You could ask the person who assigned you a login name and password (usually your system administrator), or you could ask a coworker.

What should you ask?

- What email program do people here use?

- How do I start it?

- Can you show me the most basic things that I need to know to read, send, print, and save mail?

- Is there any documentation or a help system?

- If I print something, to what printer does it go?

- What is my email address?

- Is there a list of email addresses for people at this organization?

The best way to learn the rock-bottom basics is from someone else in your environment.

What is the best feature of email?

Email keeps information moving in a timely way. You don't have to wait for artifacts like meetings or teleconferences to get your ideas out.

Linda Walsh

1

What is the best feature of email?

Convenience. I like it when my clients are on email.

I'm on the road all the time. It's almost impossible to use the phone. (Even when you're in the office, there is constant phone tag.)

Email lets me send a message and know that it will get there. I always send a copy to myself, so that if I needed to, I could resend it.

Hugh Brown

If you have a choice, choose the mailer that most people use, or that most people with your job use.

In some environments, you won't have any choice: there will be one mail system that everyone uses. In other environments, there could be a number of mailers available: simple ones or powerful ones, with graphical interfaces or command-line interfaces.

Most mailers have similar commands and capabilities. You should probably start with the program that most people use at your site. That way you'll be able to ask questions and get technical support. After you use email for a while and get used to it, you can explore other mailers at your site that might give you more power or flexibility.

If you suspect that you may have special needs, ask the person who set you up with an account on the computer for further recommendations. For example, if you are creating and sending graphic files offsite to vendors, while most others in the office are sending text files to each other, ask if you should be using a specific mailer to make life easier.

A mailer is a program; start mail like you would any other program.

You'll start the mail program in the same way that you start other programs on your computer. If you usually click on an icon or make a selection from a program menu, start your email program from there. If you start your programs from a UNIX system prompt, type the name of the program there. For example, you would type "mush" to start the mailer Mush. The following example assumes that your system prompt is a percent (%) sign:

```
% mush
```

Using a mailer is like using other applications: when you're inside the mailer, you have to use commands that the mailer understands.

As soon as you have a computer account, you're likely to start accumulating mail.

If your login account was set up some time ago, you might well have email waiting for you, especially if your name has been placed on a distribution list that receives office-wide or department-wide email.

On the other hand, you might not have any messages waiting for you to read. Some mail programs with a command-line interface might tell you that you have no mail and then quit.

```
% mush
mush: No mail for lisa
%
```

If that happens, you are no longer running the mailer, because the system prompt has come back.

All mailers show you a list of incoming messages.

Some graphical mailers start first with a main menu; you will make a choice at that menu whether you want to see the list of mail that has been sent to you, send a message, or perform other functions. Other mailers start right off by showing you the list of incoming messages; you will make a choice there to read mail, send a message, etc.

From the list of messages, you see how many messages are in the mailbox and a summary of each message. The information in the summary and the order in which it is shown can vary, but most mailers show you a message number, a message status, who the message is from, when the message was sent (or received), how big the message is, and what the subject of the message is.

You take actions from this list of message summaries.

All mailers act on the "current message" by default.

The current mail message is the selected or default message. The current message will be acted on if you don't indicate

A list of messages on a graphical mail program

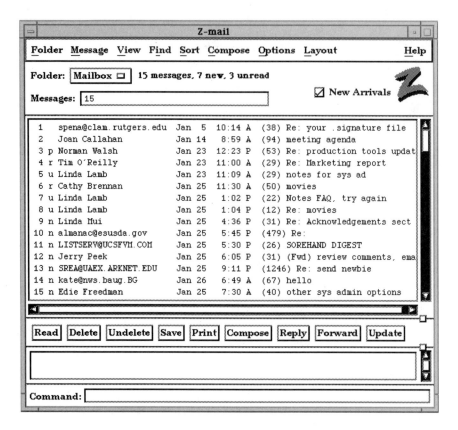

```
┌─────────────────────────── Z-mail ──────────────────────────┐
│ Folder  Message  View  Find  Sort  Compose  Options  Layout        Help │
│                                                                        │
│ Folder: │Mailbox ▢│  15 messages, 7 new, 3 unread                       │
│                                                          ☑ New Arrivals  │
│ Messages: │15                                              │            │
│                                                                        │
│    1    spena@clam.rutgers.edu  Jan  5  10:14 A  (38) Re: your .signature file │
│    2    Joan Callahan          Jan 14   8:59 A  (94) meeting agenda     │
│  3 p  Norman Walsh            Jan 23  12:23 P  (53) Re: production tools updat│
│  4 r  Tim O'Reilly           Jan 23  11:00 A  (29) Re: Marketing report │
│  5 u  Linda Lamb             Jan 23  11:09 A  (29) notes for sys ad    │
│  6 r  Cathy Brennan          Jan 25  11:30 A  (50) movies             │
│  7 u  Linda Lamb             Jan 25   1:02 P  (22) Notes FAQ, try again │
│  8 u  Linda Lamb             Jan 25   1:04 P  (12) Re: movies          │
│  9 n  Linda Mui              Jan 25   4:36 P  (31) Re: Acknowledgements sect │
│ 10 n  almanac@esusda.gov     Jan 25   5:45 P  (479) Re:               │
│ 11 n  LISTSERV@UCSFVM.COM    Jan 25   5:30 P  (26) SOREHAND DIGEST    │
│ 12 n  Jerry Peek             Jan 25   6:05 P  (31) (Fwd) review comments, ema │
│ 13 n  SREA@UAEX.ARKNET.EDU   Jan 25   9:11 P  (1246) Re: send newbie  │
│ 14 n  kate@nws.baug.BG       Jan 26   6:49 A  (67) hello              │
│ 15 n  Edie Freedman          Jan 25   7:30 A  (40) other sys admin options │
│                                                                        │
│ │Read│ │Delete│ │Undelete│ │Save│ │Print│ │Compose│ │Reply│ │Forward│ │Update│ │
│                                                                        │
│ Command: │                                                          │ │
└────────────────────────────────────────────────────────────┘
```

PC and Mac mailers are generally graphical, as are some mailers available on UNIX systems. In this book, we give examples from Eudora, cc:Mail, Pine, Elm, xmh, Z-Mail, and AOL email.

Graphical mailers have the advantage of offering a familiar interface for many people. People need to learn the terminology and the location of options under various menus, but usually are already familiar with how to make selections from menus, print, etc.

Graphical mailers typically start with a main menu. You display various screens and dialog boxes to read, send, print, or organize mail.

Some graphical programs give you icons for the most common commands. (cc:Mail has SmartIcons, where you use a single click for frequently used actions.) Some graphical programs (such as Elm or Pine on UNIX) let you use single keystrokes for menu choices, such as r for Reply.

What you need to know before you do anything else

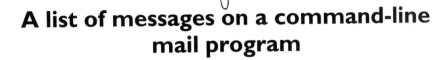

A list of messages on a command-line mail program

```
/work/iut
Frame % mush
Mail User's Shell (7.2 .0 10/31/90): Type '?'  for help.
"/usr/spool/mail/lamb": 15 messages, 7 new, 3 unread
   1    spena@clam.rutgers.edu  10:14 A 1/5/90    Re: your .signature file
   2    joan@metcom.com          8:59 A 1/14/90   meeting agenda
   3 P  norm@roa.com            12:23 P 1/23/90   Re: production tools updat
   4 R  tim@roa.com             11:00 A 1/23/90   Re: Marketing report
   5 U  lamb@roa.com            11:09 A 1/23/90   notes for sys ad
   6 R  cathy@roa.com           11:30 A 1/25/90   movies
   7 U  lamb@ora.com             1:02 P 1/25/90   Notes FAQ, try again
   8 U  lamb@ora.com             1:04 P 1/25/90   Re: movies
   9 N  lmui@roa.com             4:36 P 1/25/90   Re: Acknowledgements sect
  10 N  almanac@esusda.gov       5:45 P 1/25/90   Re:
  11 N  LISTSERV@UCSFVM.COM      5:30 P 1/25/90   SOREHAND DIGEST
  12 N  jerry@roa.com            6:05 P 1/25/90   (Fwd) review comments, ema
  13 N  SREA@UAEX.ARKNET.EDU     9:11 P 1/25/90   Re: send newbie
  14 N  kate@nws.baug.BG         6:49 A 1/26/90   hello
  15 N  edie@roa.com             7:30 A 1/26/90   other sys admin options
(7:53) lamb: #9 of 15>
```

Many mailers available on UNIX systems are command-line mailers. In this book, we give examples from Mush, Mail, Mailx, MH, and command-line Z-Mail (or Z-Mail Lite).

Command-line mailers are generally fast to use, if you are familiar with the commands and if you are comfortable running programs from a command line.

Keystrokes take less time than pulling down menus and clicking. Command-line mailers often run more quickly than graphical mailers and use fewer system resources. Command-line mailers are often very flexible and customizable (although you have to be willing to investigate your options).

Command-line mailers typically start by displaying a list of messages. You select messages to read, save, reply to, or print. You also can send mail, sort messages, etc., from the prompt line.

another message. For example, if you give the Save command without specifying a message, the mailer saves the message it considers to be the current message.

The current message in the list of messages is highlighted. In a graphical interface, the current message might be shown in reverse video (white on black); in a command-line interface, the current message might be preceded by a symbol. For example, Mush puts a right angle bracket (>) in front of the current message:

```
"/usr/spool/mail/lamb": 3 messages, 1 new, 2 unread
    1 U tim@roa.com Nov 10 8:09 Re: available next Tues
>   2 U lamb@roa.com Nov 10 8:38 meet next Thursday?
    3 N cynthia Nov 10 4:29 (33 li) Voicemail Tips
Msg #2 of 3:
```

Message 2 is the current message.

If you don't want to act on the current message, highlight another message or enter another message number in your command.

To read a message, you select it and give the read command.

Graphical mailers and command-line mailers all have Read selections or commands. Often, reading a message is considered the default action. For example, in Eudora, double-clicking on a message summary opens the message for reading. In Mush, typing a message number without any other command displays that message for reading.

When you read a message, you first see the header. The fields in the header tell you who the message is from, who the recipients of the message are, when the message was sent, and so on. The information contained in the header at the beginning of the message will be more complete than can be shown in the one-line message summary.

The header might also show technical information, such as what machines the message passed through while being routed for delivery to you. Whether or not you see these more technical details will depend on what mailer you use, how the mailer is set up at your site, and what changes you make (if any) to your environment.

What you need to know before you do anything else

Next you see the message body, which can be short (a line or two) or can go on for screens and screens. If the message is long, the mailer displays the first screenful of the message and gives you the option to read more or to quit out of the message.

When you finish reading the message, you can once again see the list of messages. At that point, you can decide to delete the message, print the message, save the message as a file, keep the message within mail, reply to the message, and so on, before considering the next message.

After you read a message, you might want to reply to it.

Mail programs have a shortcut to make replying easier. (The long way to reply would be to start a new message, type in the person's address and the same subject—so that the person receiving your reply would know that it is a reply to her earlier message.)

Mail programs have a Reply menu selection or a Reply command that automatically addresses your mail to the person who sent it and fills in the subject. Mailers commonly insert Re: in front of the subject. For example, if *arsenio@roa.com* sent you a message with the Subject: line "Tech support overwhelmed," you could use a Reply command that would address a mail message back to Arsenio's address, with a Subject: of "Re: Tech support overwhelmed." (Re: stands for regarding and is a convention that indicates a response to a previous message of the same name.) Then you would type in the message body and send it.

Mail programs let you choose between sending a reply only to the one address that the message was sent from or to the entire distribution list for that message. For example, if Arsenio sent me the message "Tech support overwhelmed" and also sent the message to Cathy and MJ, I could reply either to Arsenio only or to Arsenio, Cathy, and MJ. (With most mailers, I would also receive a copy of my reply to everyone, since I was on the original distribution list.)

There is a fine distinction between replying to one person or replying to all. Most "old hands" at email routinely double-check the To: field whenever they send a reply. For example,

Who else do you wish were on email?

I wish that all my sales accounts were on email.

Right now, 10 accounts out of 75 are on email, and they get the best service. I have an alias for those 10 accounts, and send out any new product information as soon as I get it.

Other accounts have to wait for me to be in the office and to send them faxes, etc.

I also wish my girlfriend and all my friends had email.

I have a friend in St. Louis who's on the Net. We're probably closer friends just because we can send each other email. Who has time to write a letter?

Hugh Brown

Replying

Mush, Pine, Elm, command-line Z-Mail*

r   reply to sender only

R reply to all on list

Mail*

R reply to sender only

r   reply to all on list

Eudora

Select: Reply

AOL email

Select: Reply or Reply to All

cc:Mail

Select: Reply; check or uncheck Retain the Original Addressees.

* These are the most common set-ups. However, the reply/reply-all commands might be different at your site.

in Mush, the command to reply only to the sender is r. The command to reply to everyone on the original distribution list—including yourself—is R.

Delete by indicating a message and giving the delete command.

If you won't need a message anymore, delete it. Deleting a mail message keeps your mailbox from getting too full, making it easier to find messages and saving space for messages that are really important.

The mailer actually erases the message from the mailbox only when you quit the mail program. So, if you delete a message by accident, or if you change your mind about deleting it, you can "undelete" the message at any time before you quit the mailer.

For example, with Mush, you delete message 5 by typing d, for delete:

d 5

Undelete message 5 by typing u for undelete:

u 5

Print messages the same way: select the message and give the command.

With graphical mailers, the command is usually called Print; you can set options, such as what printer to use, either in a Print dialog box or under a configuration menu.

In UNIX command-line mailers (Mail, Mailx, Mush, Z-Mail), the print command is usually lpr. Typing lpr prints the current message. Typing lpr 5 prints message number 5. For those mailers, the p command doesn't send a message to the printer; it "prints" a message on the screen.

You can save a message to a file.

There are times when you want to save the entire body of a message as a file external to the mail program. For example, you might want to save a text message as a file that you will read into a word processing program. Or, a message might contain a program that you want to save as a file and run.

To save a message as a file, you indicate the message, give the save command, and then give the filename to which you want to save the message. For example, in Eudora, select Save As and give the filename. In Mush:

```
w 6 ~/mtg.agenda
```

saves (writes) message number 6 as a file named mtg.agenda in your home directory; the file does not contain the message header, only the message body. With some mailers, the original message is automatically deleted once it is saved; if you don't want that to happen, use the undelete command on the message after you save it.

You can keep a message in message format in a mailbox or folder.

There are times that you want to save a mail message as a message. You want to keep the message and be able to access it again with that mail program. Mailers have a command for this kind of save, often called Save or Store.

Mailers have different ways of dealing with mail that you want to store. Most mailers let you create a structure of mailboxes or folders in which to store saved mail. (See Chapter 4, *What you need to know to organize saved mail.*)

Most mailers have a default mailbox or folder for mail saved as a message. For example, in Mush, the Save command without a filename saves a message to the default mailbox, called mbox:

```
s 5
```

In Elm, if you read a message and don't delete it, you are asked if you want to save that message in a folder called Received:

```
Move read messages to "received" folder? (y/n)
```

In Pine, the default folder is Saved_Messages.

In some mailers, there is no default mailbox or folder for saved messages until you create and name one.

How your mailer treats saved messages depends on the mail program and on how your site is set up. Try saving a message without a header to a file and saving a message to a mailbox or folder. Observe whether your mailer automatically deletes

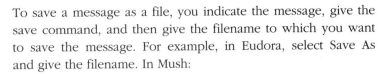

Deleting

Mush, Mail, Mailx, command-line Z-Mail, Pine, Elm

d

MH

rmm

Eudora, cc:Mail, AOL mail

Select: Delete

Example: reading and acting on messages

Mush is a command-line mailer that runs on a UNIX system. A command-line mailer is one that gives you a prompt, to which you respond with a command. Commands in Mush can be typed out fully, such as delete 2, or abbreviated to save keystrokes, such as d 2.

When you start Mush, it shows a summary of the messages in your system mailbox:

```
% mush
Mail User's Shell (7.2.0 10/31/90): Type '?' for help.
"/usr/spool/mail/jpeek":5 messages, 4 new,1 unread
  1 U eridley@metcom.com Oct 12  4:37 (169 li) GNN and re-ent
 >2 N Mitch Lee <mlee@roa Oct 13  7:32 (15 li) Call me when y
  3 N kate@nws.baug.bg Oct 13  7:58 (44 li) Request for sch
  4 N ann@funchile.cl (Ann Oct 13  8:55 (19 li) New managem
  5 N brian@roa.com Oct 13  9:07 (23 li) Re: available fo
Msg 2 of 5:
```

At the start of the list is a summary that shows the name of the mailbox and a count of messages. The list of messages displays several columns of information:

- Message number (1, 2, and so on). In this example, the second message is marked with an angle bracket (>); this is the current message.

- Status: this reminds you whether you've read a message, replied to it, and so on. The last four messages in this example have the status N for New—you've never read them. Other status abbreviations are U for Unread, R for Reply, and P for Preserved.

- Sender: the person's name and/or email address. For example, message 2 is from Mitch Lee; his address is *mlee@roa.com*. There isn't room for the entire address.

- When message was sent : The second message was sent October 13 at 7:32 AM.

- Message size. Message 2 has 15 lines.

- Message subject. (The full text of the subject is often too long to fit on the line.)

Once you see the list, you can take action on the messages. You can consider each in order, or you can skip around. If you want to read a message, type the number of that message. You'll see the message on your screen:

```
From mitch@roa.com Wed Mar 9 7:32:34 1994
Received: from roa.com by rock.west.roa.com (4.1/SMI-4.1)
  id AA28595; Wed, 9 Mar 94 7:32:32 EDT
Received: by roa.com (8.6.8/)
Message-Id: <199404091741.KAA12933@ruby>
From: Mitch Lee <mlee@roa.com>
Date: Wed, 9 Mar 1994 7:34:49 EDT
To: jpeek@roa.com
Subject: Call me when you get in

Jerry, do you read email first thing in the morning?
I'm at home with my sick daughter.
When you get this, let me know. I can email that
sales proposal we were talking about last week.
Thanks, Mitch
( Msg 2 of 5: ).
```

The top of the message is the header, with fields such as To: and From:. After a blank line comes the message body. The body can be short (a line or two) or it can go on for screens and screens. If the message is long, Mush stops after the first screenful and prints "—more—" at the bottom-left corner of the screen. At that point, you have two choices:

- To read more, press the Space or Return key.

- To quit the message without reading more, press Q.

After you read the message, you'll get another Mush prompt:

```
Msg 1 of 6:
```

Then you can give Mush commands to delete a message, reply, read another message, and so on.

What you need to know before you do anything else

For example, to delete a message, give the delete command (d) and the message number that you want to take action on (1) and then press the Return key:

   d 1

Mush recognizes the following commands (as well as many others):

d   Delete

u   Undelete

lpr Send message to printer

r   Reply to sender only

R   Reply to sender and all people on the distribution list

s   Save the message as a file

pre Preserve the message in the incoming mailbox

h   Show the list of headers

z   Page ahead to the next page of the list of headers

z-   Page back to an earlier page of the list of headers

?   See list of commands

q   Quit mail program

So, at the Mush prompt, you could print message 3:

   Msg 1 of 2: lpr 3

undelete message 1:

   Msg 1 of 2: u 1

or quit the mail program:

   Msg 1 of 2: q

My sister in California. I'd love to write letters, but I never do it.

I wish my mother was on email as well, but I know that's hopeless. She complained when my sister bought her a cassette player, "I know you're just doing this to annoy me because I could never learn to play this."

Frank Willison

saved messages and whether you have a default mailbox or folder.

Send mail by giving the mail command, typing the address of the recipient, and then typing a message.

For graphical mailers, you select a menu item or icon such as Prepare Message or Compose. For command-line mailers, you give a command to start a message. Mail, Mailx, Mush, and command-line Z-Mail use m, for mail; MH uses comp, for compose.

After you indicate that you want to send a message, you have to address the message. The mailer asks you to enter the email address of the person(s) to whom you want the message to go. Some mailers have a list of possible recipients, from which you can select names, e.g., in an address book.

Email addresses can be long or complex, especially if you exchange mail with people over computer networks. However, many times, you can exchange email with your coworkers using very simple addresses, such as login names. Ask what format you should use for email addresses within your organization. (Chapter 5 looks at more complex addressing across networks.)

For now, just ask one or two people for their email address. If you can't find anyone who uses email, you can send mail to yourself at your own email address. Type an address exactly as it's given to you; don't add spaces, punctuation, or anything you weren't specifically told to type.

You next type a subject that lets your reader know what the message is about, followed by the body of the message itself.

When you are done typing the message, you signal that you are ready to send it. For graphical mailers, you select a menu item (or icon or button) such as Send. For command-line mailers you signal with a keystroke. Mail, Mailx, Mush, and command-line Z-Mail all use the keystroke combination CTRL-D to signal that you are done composing the message and are ready to send it.

Most mailers give you a chance to reconsider sending. When you are poised to send a message, you are given a choice of cancelling (or aborting) the message, going back and re-editing the message body or headers, or going ahead and sending the message.

Mailers have editors of varying power.

What if you make a mistake as you're typing a message? Can you fix the mistake? The answer depends on the email program you're using.

Every email program (that we have seen) lets you backspace and fix a mistake on the same line. After you press Return to end a line, though, in some mailers you can't go back and fix a previous line—unless you start a smarter editor program. (We are using the term editor to mean any text-editing program that your mailer can use.)

Even if your mailer's editor is powerful enough, you might prefer to use another editor. Check the documentation or ask at your site for editors or word processors that you can use for composing mail.

Quit the mail program with another command.

Every mail program modifies your incoming mailbox when you quit the program. At that time, the mailer carries out the changes you have made: deleting messages, changing the status of messages you've read, and so on. Some mailers also let you give a command to update the mailbox while you are working in it.

With graphical mailers, select the Exit or Quit command to close the mail application. With command-line mailers, type the quit command to return to the system prompt.

For example, to leave Mush, Mail, or command-line Z-Mail, use the q (quit) command. Your system mailbox is updated if there were changes, and you are back at the system prompt:

```
Msg 2 of 2: q
Updating "/usr/spool/mail/jpeek": empty
saved 2 messages in /home/jpeek/mbox
%
```

Sending a message with Mush

I want to send mail to my friend Richard; his address is *richp@chem.ysr.edu*. I want to send the same message to my manager, whose address is *kate*.

I start the Mush program:

    mush

and a window comes up that shows me two messages. Now that I'm running Mush, I can type (at the Mush prompt at the bottom of the screen):

    m richp@chem.ysr.edu,kate

I put a comma between the two addresses. (With Mush, I could also just leave a space between the two.)

When I press Return or Enter at the end of this line, Mush starts to compose the message. It starts by making the message header . That's the part of the message that tells who it's from, where it's going, and what it's about.

Mush makes a line with To: and the email addresses I typed. Then it prompts me for the subject of the message:

    Msg 1 of 2: m richp@chem.ysr.edu,kate
    To: richp@chem.ysr.edu, kate
    Subject:

The subject lets your reader see at a glance what the message is about. Type the subject and then press Return. The cursor moves out of the header and into the first line of the message body:

    Msg 1 of 2: m richp@chem.ysr.edu,kate
    To: richp@chem.ysr.edu, kate
    Subject: Just a test message

Now you can type the text of your message. Mush uses a simple editor program for your message text. You can backspace over mistakes to erase them. When you get to the end of a line, press Return.

When you're finished typing the message, press Return once more to move the cursor to the start of a new line:

    Msg 1 of 2: m richp@chem.ysr.edu,kate
    To: richp@chem.ysr.edu, kate
    Subject: Just a test message

    Hi. I'm reading "What You Need to Know About Email" and
    sending a test email message.
    Please send me a reply. Thanks.

You don't need to sign your name, because the email system automatically adds it to the message header when it sends the message. The system also includes your email address, along with the date and time the message was sent. If you want to type your first name at the end of the message, though, to be friendly, go ahead.

To send your message, type CTRL-D at the start of a line. (Hold down the Control key and press the d key once.) You should then get another Mush prompt.

Experiment on yourself and make a few mistakes.

Experiment long enough with your mailer that you can send and read simple messages. Experiment by sending lots of mail to yourself. Reply to it. Delete it. Make spectacular mistakes in your mail to yourself. That way, you'll learn and inoculate yourself against making spectacular mistakes in mail to others.

Before you start sending out mail to other people, skim the next chapter for an idea of the kind of messages and communications that others have come to expect.

What mailer do you use?

I first used VAXmail. VAXmail is a command-line mailer that is very logical. To send mail, you type send; to see the directory of mail messages, you type dir.

VAXmail is more user friendly than UNIX mailers. The editing function within mail works in English.

I changed jobs and was working on a Mac in a networked UNIX environment. I used QuickMail for a while. Once I was used to it, mail was easy to file and find. Attaching graphic files for mailing was pretty easy. However, the server kept crashing.

Now I use Eudora. Eudora isn't that different from QuickMail. Some things were hard to get used to. By default, Eudora copies everyone on a reply. I have to remember to disable that option or to edit the address line.

Edie Freedman

Getting help with your mailer's commands

Most mailers offer some kind of online help system. There are also other sources of information, such as written documentation, UNIX manual pages (man pages), frequently-asked question (FAQ) archives, and online newsgroups.

Mail or Mailx

From within Mail or Mailx, type ? at the prompt to see the list of commands.

For an online manual page describing Mail, use the man command. At the UNIX prompt, type:

    man mail

The output of this command is many screens long. You can redirect the output to a file:

    man mail > mail.man.page

Mush

From within Mush, type ? at the prompt. This shows a list of commands. Type command –? for help with individual commands.

For example, to see how to use the display command, type:

    display -?

For the online manual page type

    man mush

This is a very long file. Most UNIX sites subscribe to many Usenet newsgroups, which are archives of online messages on various subjects. If your site subscribes, and you know how to use a news reader, you can read the Mush newsgroup, *comp.mail.mush.*

MH and xmh

    man mh

summarizes MH commands. You can get help on an individual MH command by typing the command

with the –help option. For example, to see help on the command comp, type:

    comp -help

If you know how to use a news reader, you can read a newsgroup about MH, *comp.mail.mh*, on Usenet.

If you can't read Usenet, you can subscribe to the *mh-users* mailing list. It carries the same articles as the newsgroup. To subscribe, send a mail message to *mh-users-request@ics.uci.edu.* Chapter 6, *What you need to know about mailing lists*, gives you more background about subscribing to lists.

The book, *MH & xmh: Email for Users and Programmers* (O'Reilly & Associates, Inc.), is a very comprehensive resource for using and customizing this flexible mailer.

Elm

From within Elm, type ? at the prompt to see a list of common commands. To get more information, type ? again to see the full list of commands.

You can read an FAQ (frequently asked questions) for Elm. The FAQ is posted monthly to the Usenet newsgroups *news.answers* and *comp.mail.elm.*

You can also request the Elm FAQ with an email message. Send mail to *mail-server@cs.ruu.nl* with a blank subject line and two commands in the message body:

    To: mail-server@cs.ruu.nl
    Subject:

    send NEWS.ANSWERS/elm/FAQ
    end

Pine

From within Pine, type ? to see help text. Help is part of the menu bar at the bottom of each page. Help is context-sensitive, depending on where you are in the Pine menu. For example, if you press ?

What you need to know before you do anything else

after you've selected Folders, you'll be shown information about folders, such as default folders, opening folders, renaming folders, etc.

The help messages are divided into "pages" of information to make paging through the information easier. For each help message, you can print the entire file by selecting Print once from the bottom menu.

Z-Mail

From within command-line Z-Mail, type ? at the prompt. This shows a list of commands. Type the name of a command with the −? option for help with that command. For example, to see how to use the display command, type:

display -?

Within graphical Z-Mail, click on the Help button in the upper-right corner of the screen. Click on the topic you want to see explained.

Eudora

Turn the help function on from the Balloon Help menu, selecting Show Balloons (Macintosh) or by selecting the Help option (PC). Move the cursor to a menu selection or item on the screen to display a brief description of the item.

If you have a commercial version of Eudora, you should have documentation and support available. QualComm Inc. licenses Eudora and provides support, including a printed Eudora tutorial that explains all optional settings. For the latest information about Eudora, QualComm lists an email address of *eudora-info@qualcomm.com*.

cc: Mail

Press the F1 key for a general Help index. Within a window, pressing F1 brings up a context-sensitive help message.

As a commercial product, cc:Mail comes with documentation. There are also a number of third-party books on cc:Mail.

CHAPTER 2

What you need to know to communicate well

Most people learn to write email by trial and error.

If you're the cautious type, you can learn what to avoid by noticing other people's mistakes. Object lessons abound: a private message is mistakenly sent to the whole company; a poorly-written message is misunderstood. Over time, you will notice the kinds of messages or habits that bother you, and you can vow, "*I'll* never do that."

This chapter is meant to shorten the learning-from-experience process and to help you develop an effective email style.

People who read lots of mail can be irritated by extra messages or even extra paragraphs.

If you are just starting out in email, you might get only a few messages each day. If one of those messages has a few lines more than it needs or if you get copied on a message that you don't really need to see, you probably won't think that it's any big deal.

However, many people use email as their main method of communication and get 100 or more messages a day. Keeping up with that much email is daunting.

Watching and learning

Just as there is etiquette for a conversation in person, there is etiquette for email. Email users call these manners "netiquette," short for network etiquette.

Most of my netiquette I've learned by seeing other people make mistakes: watching and learning.

Allen Noren

I saved one message that was broadcast by mistake in a file called "scandals."

Olivia Bogdan

Many people who use email also give it their highest communication priority, before telephone messages or Federal Express packages. People look in their email to see what's hot and to see what they have to take care of immediately.

When you send email, you'll want to be aware of the environment in which it will be read. Often, readers are hurrying through their mail and expect that messages will be clear, concise, and targeted to their own priorities.

Email's lack of emotional and personal context makes it best suited to factual discussions.

When you talk with someone, you can use inflection, tone, or pauses—as well as words—to get your point across. You can hear or see when another person is distressed or puzzled. If you don't understand something, you can ask a question and get a response right away.

Even when you communicate in writing, you're not dealing in words alone. Over years of written communication, we've evolved a shared "vocabulary" of form for written communications. This shared vocabulary gives the other person a context for the message.

For example, if you saw a scented, handwritten envelope slipped under your door, you would have different expectations of the message than if you saw a notice on formal stationery from a law office. And, if you saw a color advertisement on newsprint, you would have still different expectations.

Email provides less context than other methods of communicating. When you write email, it's just you and your computer screen. You have to imagine what the other person will want to know, what they'll remember about any discussion you've had before, and how they'll interpret what you write. Only the heading and text set the tone of the message.

Because of the lack of context, misunderstandings are more likely in email than with other communication methods.

There are times to use the phone instead of email.

Email isn't always the best way to communicate. When is it easier to pick up the phone?

- When you'll be negotiating, and there will be a lot of give-and-take. ("How can our two departments work better together?")
- When you want someone to respond to a series of questions that could take a long time to answer.
- When you're talking about feelings or emotionally charged subjects. ("I don't like the way you've been talking to me lately.")
- When you need an answer right away from a person who doesn't read email regularly or who tends to put it off.
- When putting it in writing could be intimidating or unfriendly.
- When you require security. A phone call or private conversation is more secure.
- When you're having a discussion with a number of people, in which everyone has input. (Have a teleconference or use discussion-group software or a bulletin board system.)

Double-check to whom you're sending mail.

One of the most common—and most embarrassing—email mistakes is sending a message to the wrong person or sending a message to more people than you intend.

This kind of mistake most often happens when you're new at email. For example, there is the employee who got an email account and started a steamy message to her paramour which began, "Now we finally have a private way to communicate...." The problem was, she mistakenly sent the message to all the hundreds of employees at the company.

After you've been using email for a while, I guarantee you'll see an example of someone being embarrassed by broadcasting a message that they meant to be private.

When do you use the phone instead of email?

Email is not good for resolving conflict; email can worsen conflict.

When I have a problem, I like to handle it in person or on the phone. You have to engage on a deeper level than merely the written word in order to come to a resolution.

Linda Walsh

If you're angry, you can whip off an angry email message and broadcast it very quickly.

Once you've used email for a while, you know better. I catch myself typing a message and then think, "Oh no, that's inappropriate." Then I reach for the phone.

Hugh Brown

Two opinions: Phone calls versus email

Email is both a blessing and a curse. It's good for some kinds of communication, but it ends up getting used for all communications.

I'm trying to restrict my own use of email to the uses it's best for.

When communicating one-on-one, I try to talk to the person—on the phone or in person—unless I need to use email for time shifting or for written records. I'll send email to a single person if:

- That person is not now available by phone
- That person (or I) will benefit from a written record of this conversation
- I am forwarding something that only exists in electronic form.

I try not to use email as a convenience only. Often that means I'm just getting something off my plate and onto someone else's.

The same goes for groups. Email can be a great way to keep a group of people "in the loop." Especially with a distributed company, this is a very important function for mail....

But if a mail discussion ever seems to be spiralling into overload, or if you seem to be developing a one-on-one argument...pick up the phone and call. Or if a lot of people are in the spin, arrange a meeting or conference call.

Tim O'Reilly

It's hard to know whether someone is available by phone until you call. If they aren't there, you end up leaving a message or calling back later. "Phone tag" is a waste of time; email avoids phone tag.

I resent getting a phone call if I can get email instead. (It's true that typing takes longer for the sender than talking would. But, for short messages, I don't think the difference is very significant.)

With a phone call, the person is forced to respond instantly... even to interrupt a conversation they're having at the time the phone call comes in. In some offices, the receptionists even page people when they aren't next to their phone, whether the call is important or not.

A phone call should be used only when something is important enough to interrupt someone from what they're doing.

If the person sends email, I can scan the email and decide whether to deal with it now or later.

When I send email, I can lay out what I'm trying to say ahead of time. I can edit my message until I'm sure that I'm explaining myself well and covering the points I want to cover.

Most people can read much faster than they can talk. So email is an efficient way to give out information.

Jerry Peek

How can such an addressing mistake happen?

- You might get interrupted while writing mail and forget to whom you originally addressed a message.

- You might reply to the wrong message number or to the wrong highlighted message.

- Or you might think that you are replying only to the sender of the message but instead be replying to the entire distribution list. Command-line mailers often use r for reply to sender and R for reply to all recipients. Graphical mailers often have one option for replying to only the sender and another option for replying to the entire group. On most mailers, the difference between the two types of replies is small enough that it is sometimes overlooked.

You can prevent these common mistakes by making it a habit to check the addresses in your message header as soon as you start a message. If you change your mind about the subject or scope of a message while you are composing, check again that the list of recipients is still appropriate.

Even if you address it right, email is still not completely private.

A person whom you don't intend to see your email message could still see it.

The person to whom you send mail could decide to forward your message to others, even if you thought the message was confidential. The person to whom you send mail could be having her mail forwarded to another employee to read while she is on a trip. Or, the person to whom you send mail could print your message, but not pick it up from the printer before someone else sees and reads it.

Even if the message goes only to the recipients you list, and no recipient lets anyone else see the message, that's not the end of the possible problems:

- Your computer, and the computers that relay your message, probably keep logs of message dates, senders and recipients.

- System backup tapes can hold copies of your mail for weeks, months, or forever.

What are your email pet peeves?

People who send mail to everyone, as a way of indicating the importance of what they are writing about.

People who send you mail for their own benefit. ("If he ever complains, I'll be able to pull out my copy of this email message and say, 'See, I told you about this two months ago.'")

People who send you a mail message with just the word "Thanks." There is some overhead involved in dealing with an email message. That overhead should not be more than the value of the message.

Frank Willison

- Networks usually aren't very secure; administrators and network "crackers" can read the data that flows down a network.

- Some U.S. courts have ruled that employers can read their employees' email without violating privacy laws.

If someone else shouldn't see your message, consider whether you should send it at all.

Think twice before sending mail.

You don't have to respond to mail immediately. If you're having a bad day or feeling very rushed, you can always save the message and think about it before replying.

Waiting and cooling off is especially important when you're angry. If you attack (or *flame*) someone else publicly on email, both of you may get hurt. Oftentimes, only the attacker ends up looking bad, losing credibility and respect as a result of his email rantings. Some organizations have rules about what is appropriate on email. (Even if there are no written rules, there are usually at least expectations of conduct.) You might be embarrassed by having to make a public apology, or you might find yourself the subject of other disciplinary action.

Address a message to the person you want to take action; copy the message to others.

When you're sending a mail message, there's more than one field where you could put a recipient's email address—To:, Cc: or Bcc:. No matter which you choose, your message will get there just the same.

When you put someone's email address in the To: field, that means the message is written to them. You're implying that you want the person to take action, to answer your questions.

When you put someone's email address in the Cc: field, that sends them a "carbon copy," or "courtesy copy," of your message. You're implying that your message is for this person's information. They can answer if they want to, but you aren't asking them to. People often send a carbon copy of a message to themselves, to keep on file.

If you put someone's email address in the Bcc: field, that person will get a blind copy of the message. Other recipients listed on the To: and Cc: fields can't tell who got blind copies, since the Bcc: field is removed before the message is sent.

There can be exceptions to this secrecy with some mail transport systems. If you want to be absolutely sure that other recipients don't see who's getting a blind copy, send a copy to yourself. Then forward your copy individually to each blind-copy recipient.

Keep headers short and descriptive.

People often select which messages to read first by their headers. If you had 100 email messages, and two minutes before a meeting was to start, which of these two would you read?

```
> 1 N Mitch Lee <mlee@roa.com> "message"
  2 N Andy Oreo <anoreo@rock.w "Urgent parts shortage"
```

Unless Mitch Lee is your boss or unless you've been waiting for a specific message from him, you'll probably pick the message with the header that sounds specific and time-critical.

Always give your message a short, descriptive subject that people can scan for. If a subject is long, make the first few words count, because anything after these first words may not be shown on the screen. Make sure the subject accurately reflects the message contents.

If messages are on the same topic, their subjects should be the same.

An email discussion, or *thread*, is a lot easier to follow if all the messages have the same Subject: field.

Generally, keep the same Subject: field when replying to a message. When you use a reply command to respond to a mail message, mailers automatically use the same Subject: header, often first inserting a Re: (for Regarding) in front of the subject. For example, suppose that a salesperson had sent out a message about a presentation:

```
Subject: Presentation to Acme
```

What is your email pet peeve?

The way that people use email.

Too many people copy too many people on stupid stuff. Or, they reply to everyone instead of replying to sender only.

Everyone makes mistakes sometimes, but some people make mistakes all the time.

Edie Freedman

Replies to that message would have the same Subject: with Re: inserted:

```
Subject: Re: Presentation to Acme
```

The topic of a discussion can change. For example, if you wanted to branch off into a discussion of a related topic mentioned in the report on the Acme presentation, you should change the Subject: field:

```
Subject: Delivery problems
```

If there has been an ongoing discussion on a different topic, you might want to include the subject of the first discussion in the new subject, like this:

```
Subject: Delivery problems (was: Presentation to Acme)
```

That lets people follow the discussion thread when they scan their message subjects.

Give the context for your reply by quoting from the original message.

Often, it makes good sense to include a previous message in your own reply:

- To remind recipients what was already said and to set the context for your reply

- To widen a discussion and catch up new recipients on the pertinent discussion so far

You can paraphrase and summarize a previous message (if the point was simple).

Or you can quote the sender exactly. The email convention for including a message is to introduce the inclusion and to mark it off from the rest of the text. Each included line is usually preceded by a symbol, such as the greater than sign (>), so that the recipient can tell where the included message ends and your response begins:

```
On Aug 21st at 9:00, Arsenio Santos wrote:
>  Because we have so many conflicting opinions
>  on this project, I think that we should take
>  the discussion "off-line."

I agree. Dale, since you, Arsenio and I need to agree
whether to go forward, let's get on the phone to discuss it.
```

What you need to know to communicate well

```
I'll set up a conference call. Is Tuesday at 10 your time
alright?
--
Linda
```

It is a good idea to skip a line any time you introduce quoted material or start your reply.

When you tell your mailer to include a previous message, only the body of the message is included, along with a line that tells who sent the original message. Unless the included message is very short and to the point, you should edit the message, to include only the text that is needed.

(If you're looking up the particulars of including messages on a help system, here is a hint on terminology: some UNIX mailers use the term *forwarding* to refer both to forwarding a message to another user and to including messages.)

Email Golden Rule: See your message through the reader's eyes.

When you write a message, try to see your reader's point of view:

- Are you composing a message to a group of people? Does a large part of your message apply only to one of those people? If so, you might split that large part into a separate email message. That way, your recipients will get only the part of the message that applies to them.

- Are you writing short, summary-type messages for people who don't want to know the details and including details for people who can handle them? You could send a summary mail message to everyone and send a follow-up message with more details to those people who need the details.

- Are you matching the tone to your audience? If some of the recipients are formal, including cute asides and graphics within your message will make you look unprofessional. On the other hand, if your recipients are a wide audience on the Internet, writing too formally might make you look unfriendly or stiff.

Include the current message in your reply

Mush, command-line Z-Mail:

While composing the message, type the include command at the beginning of the line:

~i

You can also name a message to include by number:

~i 10

Eudora

Choose Reply from the Message menu.

Z-Mail

While in Compose, click on Include.

Elm, Pine

Type r to reply to message. Elm or Pine asks you if you want to include a copy of the message.

cc:Mail

Click on the Reply Smart-Icon. In the dialog box, choose whether or not to Retain the Original Items (include the message and attachments).

Including messages within my messages

Context is really important in email, especially when you're including part or all of another message.

If I am including another message and breaking it up to reply to different parts, I start my message with text like this: "I've included comments below on several parts of your message." Also, I add a blank line or two before and after each one of my comments. This helps my comments stand out so the reader can find them easily.

When including part of another message in my message, I try to include no more and no less of the original message than the reader needs to understand the context. I consider both the time interval and the reader's understanding.

If I am having a rapid exchange of messages during a brief period of time about a subject that is well understood, I don't need to provide much context. The exchange is happening in "real time" like a conversation; I don't need to keep saying, "This is what we're talking about."

However, if I have not communicated with the recipient recently—or at all—about the topic of the included message, I include more of the original message in order to provide context.

Sometimes it's necessary, for the sake of context, to include many parts of an email chain along with my response. For example, I was reviewing a contract recently, and wanted to include a brief history of several people's responses on different points. To avoid confusion, I added text such as: "Lisa said:" or "Tim replied:" before the relevant person's comments, and prefaced my comments with: "My new comment." This might sound tedious, but it helps the reader to understand who said what when.

Some people add text to an included message at the top of the original message, and others add text at the bottom of the message. (This is sometimes determined by the mail program.)

The rule of thumb I use: if I am coming in on an email discussion, I follow the convention (text added above or below) that is already established. If I am the first person responding to a message that I am including, then I add the text where it will make the most sense to the reader.

Gina Blaber

Make response to your email easy by making your questions easy to find.

If you need an answer from someone, don't bury your question in the middle of a long message. If the message is complicated or long, start the message with a summary of what you'll be asking and what you need. Make the question stand out—probably in a separate paragraph at the end. If you have a deadline, state it.

Don't SHOUT with caps.

If you type mail in all capital letters, this gives the effect of "shouting" on the keyboard.

```
To: CATHY
Subject: THERMOSTAT

CAN'T WE DO SOMETHING ABOUT THE THERMOSTATS? PEOPLE KEEP
TURNING THEM UP HIGH TO GET "WARMER, QUICKER." DON'T THEY
KNOW THAT A THERMOSTAT JUST UNDERSTANDS ON AND OFF? IF THEY
SET THE THERMOSTAT UP TO 80, THAT JUST MAKES THE FURNACE RUN
LONGER UNTIL THE BUILDING GETS TOO HOT. WHAT'S WRONG WITH
THESE PEOPLE??
```

People will perceive you as being heavy-handed or rude.

If your message is in all caps, it is also harder to read. Text written in all caps has less "texture" (recognizable outlines) and other cues than text in mixed case. People have to read more slowly to make sense of the message.

If your computer system forces you to type commands in uppercase letters, remember to disengage your Caps Lock key before composing an email message.

Some email users don't capitalize anything. The lack of capitals also makes reading more difficult.

Don't use the tab key to indent text or make columns.

Why not use the tab key? Your mail probably won't read the same way on other machines as it does on yours:

- People who read your message may have tab stops set at different columns than you do.

Linda Lamb

- If people quote your message in a reply, tab characters in your message can cause strange indentations in their reply.
- Some mail transport agents turn tabs into single spaces.

A maximum line length for messages is about 60 characters

Although the "standard" computer window is 80 characters across, many people have windows that display fewer than 80 characters. If your lines are longer than can be shown on someone else's screen, each line of your mail will be broken into two lines: one long line followed by a short stub on the next line.

If people quote your text in a reply, they'll need room for the email program to insert characters like > in the left margin. People may requote quoted sections; it's not unusual to see two or even three layers of indents (>>).

If your email program doesn't have *word wrap*, which formats your text automatically, remember to press Return at the end of each line. If you have a computer window that's wider than the standard 80 characters, think about resizing it to 80 (or 60) so that you'll remember to press Return to end a line.

Use white space to make your message easier to read

You don't have many formatting tools available when you are writing email. Don't overlook the effective use of white space (blank lines and indents).

Break long paragraphs into shorter ones, so that the text is easier to read. Put a blank line between paragraphs, to prevent your message from looking like a wall of text with no breaks. This is especially true when you're quoting someone else's message: put a blank line between the quoted section and your reply.

One good way to break up complicated information is to make a list. Start each new point with a number or a "bullet" such as a dash or an asterisk. If a point is longer than a single line, indent the continuation lines.

What you need to know to communicate well

Practice active reading

You can find out a lot by reading your email for its communication style as well as its content.

While you're learning email, copy yourself on every message that you send out. What do you see that is different from what you expected to see? Reading your own mail is also a good way to become aware of some default settings that you might not otherwise know about.

Evaluate messages from other people in a similar fashion. What messages do you get that don't apply to you? Should they have been addressed differently? Why do you think that the sender addressed the message that way? What messages are easy for you to understand? What messages are confusing? What reasons can you see for the difference?

If you find a coworker whose mail is clear, concise, and a pleasure to read, ask him for advice on your email writing. Tell him that you're learning email style and would like to find how to communicate like he does. Copy him on a few messages and ask how the messages might be improved.

If part of your job is to give regular email reports to others, ask those recipients what kind of information they want to see and how they want it summarized. Sometimes people really want to see far fewer details than you feel obliged to supply.

Resources

Netiquette

A humorous description of Net manners can be read online in the Emily Postnews posting. Here are several ways to get a copy, depending on what software you have access to:

- If you have a World Wide Web browser, go to the URL:

    ```
    http://www.cis.ohio-state.edu/hypertext/fax/usenet
        /emily-postnews/part1/faq.html
    ```

- If you have access to the Usenet newsgroups, look in the group *news.announce.newusers* or *news.answers*.

- If you have FTP access, FTP to the archive of answers postings on *rtfm.mit.edu*, and look in */pub/usenet/news.answers*.

Privacy

If you're interested in finding out more about privacy in email, and on the Internet in general, there is an FAQ on this subject.

- If you have a World Wide Web browser, go to the URL:

  ```
  http://www.cis.ohio-state.edu/hypertext/fax/usenet
        /net-privacy/top.html
  ```

- If you can read Usenet, look in *news.announce.newusers* or *news.answers* for the posting with the subject net-privacy.

CHAPTER 3

What you need to know to be productive

You can get bogged down by email, just as you can get bogged down by phone calls or paperwork.

If you are receiving and sending lots of messages, email can start to feel like a burden. You might still be glad to see most messages. But some days, it can feel like you spend too much time getting through your email; it can feel like email *is* your job.

This chapter shows you ideas for productively processing the mail you get, so that you can get on to the rest of your work.

Look at how you're using mail.

There is no one "right" way to use email or to be productive. But if you are feeling that email is controlling you, rather than the other way around, expand the way that you're looking at the problem.

Here are some of the kinds of questions you might ask yourself:

- Should you be using the phone? Some decisions or discussions take longer if they're conducted by email.

- Should email be the online format for this information? Maybe you know that you want to have certain facts online, but email—with its implied characteristics of timeliness and

Keeping up with email

I get about 50 messages a day and leave very few overnight. I usually come in in the morning to find about 20 messages that were sent from the West coast, late the day before.

A few weeks ago, I worked late on Friday and got my messages down to zero. When I came back in Monday at 8 am, I found that I had 45 messages—most from two editors who had worked over the weekend.

That was a little discouraging. If I work until 7 PM on Friday, I should be able to have a little slack the next Monday.

Frank
Willison

sequence—might be the wrong format. Other options might be to set up a discussion group or newsgroup or to archive the information in a file or database that can be referred to as needed. Check with a system administrator for ideas on available tools or formats.

- Do people in your company or group have similar expectations of email? This question can lead to others: How do you train new users about email usage within your company? Who gives feedback to users? Are most people overwhelmed by too many messages and too much information? How do people find out about what's happening in other parts of the organization?

- Are you getting the information you want from the messages you read? If you don't need to see the mail sent to a group of people, ask to be taken off the list. If you are overwhelmed by constant updates on the details of a project, ask to see only a weekly summary.

- How often do you read mail? Although mail can feel compelling and urgent, you can choose to read mail only several times a day, to cut down on interruptions.

The online help system is a source of productivity ideas and how-to.

Depending on which mail program you use, online help can prompt you for actions the mailer is expecting, remind you of the names of commands, or list options for commands. Some online help systems give you descriptions of more general topics.

If a mailer is freely available and in the public domain, there is usually someone who maintains an FAQ list (frequently asked questions) online. If a mailer is commercial, the manufacturer has hopefully done a good job documenting its features.

If you're not familiar with help resources for your mailer, ask your coworkers or your system administrator. The two-page listing in Chapter 1, *What you need to know before you do anything else*, briefly describes the help program for sample mail programs, as well as other sources of information such as software providers, mailing lists, and Usenet newsgroups. You'll also want to check to see if printed documentation or a manual is available for the mailer.

How do you handle a large amount of mail?

I try to read in sequence. If I don't, I don't deal with all my messages. I read each one, then delete, save, or—for a small number—follow up.

When I read mail in the office, I start reading with the first new messages. Right now I have 130 messages, 25 new. (I get about 10 or so an hour.)

When I'm away on business, I usually have a small window of time in which to read email. When I only have a limited time, I skip around in reading. I try to pick the most important or pressing messages.

If I've been away, I pick messages by low priority and delete unread.

Tim O'Reilly

I just read mail sequentially.

I manage an electronic travel resource center. I get a lot of mail from people I don't know, on subjects that I won't understand until I get into the message itself. With so many unknowns, I can't sort my mail and act on messages as a group.

My productivity hint? Get to it. If I leave messages sitting, I don't get to them.

Allen Noren

When I've been away and have a lot of mail, I first look for all the messages I can delete and get rid of them quickly. For example, I dump all the messages from the LA Lakers mail list that I'm on (about five a day).

Hugh Brown

I'm one of two people who answer mail sent to a technical support address. The mail comes in waves. When I look at a large "lump" of separate problems, I attack it in two steps.

1. On the first pass, I look for all questions I can answer quickly, say in 20 keystrokes or less. I only want to look at that mail one time. Those kind of responses are generally Yes-No answers or answers that we have automated—for example, someone wants an online catalog or ftp instructions.

2. The second pass is for questions that need research. Some research doesn't take more than a few minutes, for example if I just have to look something up in a book. Other times, I might have to wait days to resolve a question, for example if I need to send queries to other people and wait for them to respond.

When I do have a backlog, I try to work first on the oldest request.

Mary Jane
Caswell-Stephenson

Mailers let you sort message headers by date, subject, author, etc.

Most mail programs store incoming messages in a single text file. (Mail, Mailx, Mush, Z-Mail, Pine, Elm, Eudora, and cc:Mail all work this way.) As new messages come in, they are added to the end of that file, in the order in which they are received.

When you start a mail program, the mailer displays a list that summarizes each message in that file. (The information for this summary list is taken from each message's header.) By default, most mailers are set to display messages in the order in which they are received.

In many mailers, you can change the order in which the messages are shown while you are reading mail. You can usually sort by some or all of the header fields—Date:, To:, From:, Subject:.

When you have more mail in your inbox or in a folder than you can scan at one glance, you might want to:

- Sort by Date: to reorder the messages in a mail folder by the date and time they were sent

- Sort by From: (or Sender:) to group the messages sent by a single person

- Sort by To: to group messages sent to a mailing list to which you subscribe or to a system list of which you are a member

- Sort by Subject: to find a message and all of its replies. Mailers generally ignore Re: at the start of the subject, so this sort groups replies with the original message.

- Sort ignoring case. Some mailers differentiate between uppercase letters and lowercase letters by default. That is, a message with the subject "Lunch at noon?" might not sort together with "lunch at noon?" For example, with command-line Z-Mail or Mush, you need to specify a –i option to sort ignoring case.

  Other mailers ignore case by default. For example, with Eudora, you select the Match Case option to match the case of your search word.

- Sort by message status. Some mailers will sort by message status. For example, with Mush, you do this by typing only sort with no other option. New messages are listed first, preserved messages are next, and deleted messages are last. If you've skipped through your mail, reading some messages and leaving some for later, sorting this way can make mail reading easier.

You can act on a group of messages at one time.

With Eudora, cc:Mail, and other mailers with graphical interfaces, you can mark a group of messages by highlighting them; then you can act on the entire group with a single command.

With some mailers (including all command-line mailers), you can act on messages by number. You can indicate a group of messages by number and act on the group at one time. For example, in the mailer Mush, to delete messages 5, 6, 8, and 10, type:

d 5 6 8 10

You can also delete a range of messages:

d 5-10

You can locate mail messages in which a word or phrase appears.

You can use a word search to select all messages that deal with a single discussion, to read them sequentially. You can search for the word or phrase within message subjects only. You can also search for the word or phrase within the entire message text of all messages. Usually, the search is restricted to the current mailbox or folder.

Your mailer will have search defaults. By default, some mailers search by the header's Subject field; some mailers search through all the text of both message body and header. Some mailers match both text and case; some search ignoring case. (Ignoring case means that if you search for the word "safety," both safety and Safety will match.)

With graphical mailers, searches generally show you one match at a time. Command-line mailers generally show you the list of all messages that match your search.

With many UNIX mailers, you can search for a set of messages and then act on those messages as a group. You can use the

Sorting commands and options

Mush, command-line Z-Mail

Command: sort

Options: date, subject, from, to, status, ignore case

Eudora

Select: Sort from the Edit menu.

Options: priority, status, sender, date subject

Elm

Select: Sorting criteria from the Options menu

Options: date mail received, date mail sent, message sender, lines in message, subject, status, mailbox order

cc:Mail

Select: Lists from the File menu

Options: date sent, last message first or first message first

MH

Command: sortm

Options: any date, any date range, any header field, or combination of two selections pipe command to pass the results of a search command to another command. For example, you could search for all messages with safety in their subjects and then delete those messages. In Elm this command would be:

```
//safety | d
```

In Mush or command-line Z-Mail, this would be:

```
pick -s safety | d
```

(The sidebar "Using the pick command with Mush and Z-Mail" shows more ways to use the pick command in Mush.)

You can forward (or resend) mail to another person, as if it were sent to them by the original sender.

Sometimes you get a message that should really go to someone else. A message could have been sent to you by mistake. Or, someone else knows the answer to the question being asked and should reply directly to the sender.

Mailers let you forward mail to another address. For example, cc:Mail has a Forward selection. In Mush, the command:

```
mail -f joan
```

forwards the current message to the user named *joan*.

When you forward a mail message, the message appears as if it came from the original sender. When the recipient reads the message, she'll see some Resent: fields that get added when you forward a message. The Resent: fields are handy, because the recipient can tell how the message got to her mailbox.

When a recipient of a forwarded message replies to that message, her reply goes to the original sender.

When you forward a message to another person, the message is not automatically deleted from your mailbox.

Deleting is key to good mail housekeeping.

The more messages you keep in a mailbox, the harder your mail is to handle. If you have hundreds of messages, it will take you longer to open the mailbox, find a message, or know what's in there. Messages relentlessly flow into your inbox.

Even if you receive only 15 messages a day, in three weeks that's over 300 email messages.

Many mail messages are just fleeting reminders of one-time notes. "Meeting changed to 2 PM." "What do you think of this idea?" As with paper that crosses your desk, you don't want to reread all your messages several times before deciding what to do with them. You can read and discard many messages immediately.

If your mailbox does get full, and you go back through the messages, you will probably be amazed at the things you saved. "Why would I want to hang on to that?" One skill needed to stay on top of your mail is to decide what you really need to save and then delete the rest fearlessly.

Look for messages you can quickly delete.

When you're trying to boost productivity, look for ways that you can streamline deletions and spend less time on each message:

- Delete as soon as you read the message, or as you are saving it or printing it.

- Delete messages on topics that don't apply to you. For example, if you see "Out on Tuesday" as the subject of mail from a colleague, you might feel comfortable deleting the message unread, unless your job requires you to track this person's schedule. Or, if you've received 11 messages about a networking problem, and you decide—after reading the first message—that you don't need to follow this discussion, delete all 11 messages at one time.

- Delete by sender or by a combination of sender and subject. If you've decided that you don't have time to read the mail that you get from a certain alias or mailing list while you're on deadline, you can delete by sender.

- Delete by date received. You can decide that any mail older than a month should be deleted. Or you can put question-able messages in a folder named for the month. After a month or two, delete the folder.

Using the pick command with Mush and Z-Mail

With Mush or Z-Mail, you can not only sort messages by header fields—To:, From:, or Priority:—you can pick them out and display only those messages.

Basic pick options

Suppose that you are looking for one or more messages that talk about safety training.

If you want to check for the word "safety" in any message in the mailbox—whether the word occurs in a header or within the message—use pick without an option:

> pick safety

If you want to make the same search for the phrase "safety training", use quotation marks to indicate more than one word:

> pick "safety training"

or use the —e option to indicate that what follows is a phrase:

> pick -e safety training

If you want to search only the Subject: field for a word, use the —s option:

> pick -s safety

By default, pick is case-sensitive. If you search for "safety," you will not see matches of "Safety." If you want to search ignoring case—and match both safety and Safety—you need to use the —i option:

> pick -si Safety

You can also pick messages from an author:

> pick -f brian

You can pick the last two messages on a given subject:

> pick -2 -s Safety

There are many other pick options. To see the entire list, type:

> pick -?

A favorite time-saver: acting on "picked" messages as a group

pick is often a favorite command for Mush or Z-Mail users, because you can select all messages containing a certain pattern and act on them as a group. How does pick come in handy?

1. You want to clean out all messages more than two months old.

   The command to list messages sent more than two months ago is:

   > pick -ago -2m

   This gives you a list of the messages.

   You can use a vertical bar (|) to join Mush or Z-Mail commands. (If you've used pipes in UNIX, this is sort of the same idea. But, in Mush, the vertical bar only sends message numbers—instead of all the output of the pick command.)

   If you want to delete the messages, add a vertical bar and the d command:

   > pick -ago -2m | d

   If you make a mistake picking messages to delete, you can undelete them in the same way:

   > pick -ago -2m | undelete

2. You'd like to save all messages from a discussion into a folder called project.

   Suppose that you want to save a number of messages that have the subject "Next project for 1994" (and "Re: Next project for 1994"). You can use a shortcut, and search for "Next project" if you're sure that other messages don't have a subject that contains that phrase. Searching for those two words, you can pick by subject and then save the matching messages to a folder:

   > pick -s "Next project" | s +project
   > Saving msg 4 ... (17 lines)
   > Saving msg 17 ... (46 lines)

```
Saving msg 33 ... (99 lines)
Appended 3 msgs to ~/Mail/project
```

3. You're on a lot of mailing lists, and you're trying to find the messages you mailed to a particular list.

   To figure out how to pick out messages from a mailing list, you need to read a few of the old messages to see if they have some header field in common. For example, messages sent by List-proc to the *ora-news* mailing list all have a field that looks like this:

   ```
   Originator: ora-news@online.ora.com
   ```

   You can search for all messages that contain "ora-news" in the header field Originator:

   ```
   pick -h originator "ora-news"
   ```

   As another example, messages sent by Listserv from the *mud-w* mailing list have a header like this:

   ```
   Sender: Mud Wrestling Fanatics <MUD-W@GONZO.USYR.EDU>
   ```

   So to find all messages sent to the *mud-w* list, you can search for all messages that contain *mud-w* in the field Sender:

   ```
   pick -h sender "MUD-W"
   ```

4. You're on mailing lists, and your system mailbox is full of list mail that you don't want to read right now.

   In this case, you'd like to find only that mail sent directly to you (that is, mail not sent from mailing lists).

   Most mailing lists don't put your address in the To: field. They put your address in the message envelope, which is invisible to most email users; only the computer sees it.

   So, you can filter out mail from mailing lists by searching for mail that contains your address in the To: header:

   ```
   pick -t "jerry"
   ```

Know the default actions your mailer takes on messages you've read.

As a default, some mailers automatically delete messages that you have read if you don't specifically save or preserve them. Many people like this automatic deletion; it keeps their mailboxes clean without much effort on their part.

However, your mailer might act differently (either because of the defaults of that mailer or because your system administrator has set the defaults differently at your site). The default at your site might be to keep all messages unless you specifically delete them. If you read a message and take no action, your mailer might automatically save it to another mailbox of read mail, or it might automatically preserve messages in your incoming mailbox.

Part of being productive is knowing what happens if you do nothing. Observe what happens when you read, but don't delete, a few unimportant messages. Do they disappear from your inbox after you leave the mail program? Are they saved in a folder of old mail messages?

If you don't like the default settings, you can probably change them to match your wishes. See Chapter 8, *What you need to know to show off.*

You can copy a file into a mail message.

Almost all mailers let you "read in" a file to your message. That way, you can read in any file that you have prepared with another editor on your system. You'll want to make sure that the files are ASCII files—text only, with no other formatting. (Chapter 9, *What you need to know to send files*, talks about sending other kinds of files in mail.)

Reading in files is handy when you want to write a message ahead of time and send it later, or when you've already saved text in a file. For example, you might frequently send out the same information in response to email inquiries. If so, you can put the text into a file and read that text file into an email message whenever it's needed.

You can use your favorite text editor within many mail programs.

Mailers have their own editor. Often this editor is not sufficient for your needs, if you communicate a lot through email. For example, some editors are so simple that you have to backspace over everything you've typed and then retype it.

With many mailers, you can give a program command to start another editor, or you can set the default mail editor to be your favorite editor.

You can use any editor that can save your mail message as a plain ASCII file that has no formatting except linebreaks at the right margin.

Some mailers support other commands, like those that list files or lock your keyboard.

Aside from the basic commands for reading, organizing, and sending mail, mailers let you print messages and ask for help. They also offer other "housekeeping" commands that you might need while processing your mail.

The "other" commands offered by different mailers vary. For example, within Pine, you can change your password, lock your keyboard, or show the space left on your disk. Within Eudora on a Macintosh, you can see the files in folders, change passwords, empty trash, compact mailboxes, save a message for later transmission, and create or change nicknames (aliases). Within Mush, you can list files and change directories.

To run other commands while you are in mail, you need multiple windows or a system prompt.

When you are in mail, you often want to run a command that is not strictly related to mail. For example, you might want to copy a text file into your mail message, but not be able to remember the exact name of the file. In that case, you would like to quickly list the contents of a directory to check on the filename, so you can copy in that file and then continue with

Using an editor within a UNIX mailer

Two common UNIX editors are vi and Emacs. Your system administrator may have set your UNIX mailer to start a particular editor.

To start the editor while you're sending a mail message, use the ~v command while you're composing a message body (after you've filled in the addresses and the subject). You must be at the beginning of a line when you use ~v.

After you type ~v (and press Return, of course), your text editor will start. If you've typed anything into the message body, you'll see that text from inside the editor. Otherwise, just start typing the message body. Don't add italics, highlighting, or anything but text into your file (unless you're using a MIME-compliant mailer, as discussed in Chapter 9, *What you need to know to send files*).

When you're done, save the file and quit the editor. You'll be back inside the mailer. If you're happy with the message you composed in the editor, send it as usual.

When using another editor inside a command-line mail program, some people find it hard to remember "where they are."

If you use both the mailer's editor and your own editor, occasionally you might be confused. When you're typing a message, are you using the mail program's editor or another editor? What commands will work? Where are you?

It may help to think of sending mail and using an editor as a four-step process. You start two programs, so you have to end two programs. Some people think of using an editor as "dropping down into the editor" as a model to help them remember their place.

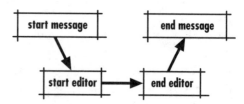

If you keep using the editor, you'll get practiced at knowing where you are. When you don't remember, you can look at the screen for clues.

If you're in the vi editor, for instance, lines after the end of the file are marked with tildes (~) at the left-hand margin.

Another way to find out is to give a command that will tell you where you are (without hurting the message). For example, if you think you're in vi, the CTRL-g command displays the filename and size. If you think you're in the mailer, you can try the help command, such as ~?.

What you need to know to be productive

the message. Sometimes you can run such a command within your mailer; sometimes the mailer won't support the command you would like to use.

What can you do if you need to run a command that your mailer doesn't support? It is inconvenient to quit the mail program, run the command, then start your mail program again and get back to where you were.

If you have multiple windows on your computer, you can run the command in another window, to get around the restrictions of your mailer.

Most UNIX mailers, like Mush and Z-Mail, have a shell escape the sh command, which lets you start a UNIX shell (you usually get a $ or % prompt). You can then run some commands and return to the mail program. If you use Mail, you can issue a single UNIX command by typing ! followed by the command:

```
&!date
Mon Mar 13 13:21:32 EST 1995
!
&
```

Or you can type:

```
&!sh
```

to start a shell. In any case, you won't lose your place in the mail program; when you leave the shell, you'll be right back where you were. (You use MH commands from the shell, so MH doesn't need a shell escape.)

Or, if you're composing mail with a UNIX editor such as vi or Emacs, you can access UNIX commands with a shell escape from within the editor.

If you've stopped or dropped out of your mail program temporarily, remember to go back to the same session instead of starting a new one. That is, if you start Mush and use the sh command to start a new shell, don't type mush again to get back into Mush! If you do, you'll have two sessions (one stopped, the other running) and your mail can get mixed up.

Aliases can save time in looking up names and typing addresses.

An alias is another name for something. In email, an alias is an address created for convenience so that you don't have to type

Copying a file into a mail message

cc:Mail

Select: Attach from the Message menu

Mush, Mail, Mailx, command-line Z-Mail

At the beginning of a line, enter:

~r *filename*

while composing a message. For example, to read in the file examples, type:

~r *examples*

If you are in another editor, use that editor's command for reading in a file.

Pine

Hold down the Control key, press r, and then type the filename:

CTRL-R *filename*

long lists of individual names or so that you don't have to remember complicated addresses.

There are two types of aliases: systemwide aliases and personal aliases.

A systemwide alias is created by a system administrator (or mail administrator) for the convenience of everyone on the system. System aliases can be used by anyone.

A personal alias is created by you for your own convenience and can only be used by you. Personal aliases can also be called Nicknames, Mailing Lists, Address Books, Notebooks, etc., depending on which mailer you use.

Be aware of company-wide system aliases.

System aliases, created by your system administrator, might be:

- **Required.** For example, computers connected to the Internet are required to have a *postmaster* address, so that mail can be delivered to the person in charge of the email system on that computer. Having a standard *postmaster* address allows people to know where to send their questions and allows mailing programs to have a place to send error messages.

- **Requested by people in the company, for groups to communicate with each other.** For example, departments might each have their own alias, such as *sales*. The *sales* alias would include the individual email addresses of each person in the sales department. If you want to send out a message to a group of people who shared a function or interest, you do not need to keep track of everyone's individual address; you can send mail to the alias, and it will be routed automatically.

- **Administrative.** A system administrator can create aliases to make things easier for email users. For example, Sun Microsystems assigns an alias to every user, with the format of Firstname.Lastname. That way, if you know a person's name, you can get email to him or her.

  As another example, a system administrator can create an alias for someone whose address is frequently misspelled or misdirected, so that mail sent to the commonly mistaken address still gets delivered.

What you need to know to be productive

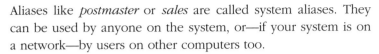

Aliases like *postmaster* or *sales* are called system aliases. They can be used by anyone on the system, or—if your system is on a network—by users on other computers too.

When you use a system alias, that address stays in the message header that other people receive. For example, if you send email to the system alias *sales*, recipients see *sales* in the To: field.

On some computer systems, if you are on a system alias, you may not get a copy of messages you send to that alias. For example, if you are on the *sales* alias and send a message to *sales*, you might not receive a copy unless you specifically remember to copy yourself.

On UNIX systems, the list of system aliases may be available with the ypcat command:

```
ypcat mail aliases
```

Or you may be able to look at the list in the file /usr/lib/ aliases. On some UNIX systems, you can use the verify command to see who is listed for an alias (see Chapter 5, *What you need to know to send mail over networks*).

You can create personal aliases for your own use.

Do you frequently send mail to the same group of people? Maybe four of you get together for lunch every week and you're the one who picks the place. Instead of typing four email addresses each week, you can make an alias named *lunch* and send mail to that alias. Or, maybe you send mail to someone who has an email address that's long or hard to remember. You can make an alias for that person.

When you send mail to a personal alias, the address is converted to the individual addresses as the message is sent. For example, if you send mail to a *lunch* alias of four people, each person sees a message from you, addressed to them and to the three others on the list.

When you create a personal alias, you're the only one who can use the alias.

If you make a personal alias, try to avoid using an address already in use on your system. For example, let's say you make an alias named *joan* for your friend Joan in England. If some-

Creating a personal alias

Mush, command-line Z-Mail, Mail, Mailx, Elm, Pine

Edit the .rc file for your mailer, in your home directory (.mailrc, .mushrc, .zmailrc, .mailxrc, .elm/elmrc, or .pinerc. The list command ls –a shows you the hidden "dot" files or directories.)

To create the alias, enter a line in the format:

alias *newname fulladdress*

For example, to create an alias for the address *kate@nws.baug.bg*, enter the line:

alias kate kate@nws.baug.bg

Eudora

Select: Nicknames from the Special menu; add new aliases with the New button.

cc:Mail

Select: Private Mailing Lists from the Select menu; enter new mailing list name and addresses.

Message priorities

Elm

If you put any value in the Priority: field—other than normal or non-urgent)—Elm puts a U by the field to note the message as Urgent.

In Elm, you can also use the Action: field to indicate action for the recipient to take, or use the Expire: field to indicate a date for the mail to expire.

Eudora

There are five levels of priority that you can assign to a message when it is sent. Level 1 is most urgent and is shown as ++ in the list of message headers.

cc:Mail

While you are composing in a New Message window, open the Priority menu. Select Low, Normal, or Urgent.

one in your company has the email address *joan,* too, you won't be able to send mail to her without specifying her full mail address; mail sent to *joan* will always go to your friend Joan in England.

Most mailers let you assign priorities to messages that you send.

Assigning a priority to a message is a way that you can indicate to a recipient that your message is important and needs to be read soon. Some people sort their mail by priority. Most mailers have a space where an "urgent" mark can appear when messages are displayed.

Of course you can also indicate importance or timeliness of a message in the Subject: itself.

```
10  Today, meeting at 2:00
11  Important: need to talk about trade show
```

You only want to label your message as important or urgent when it needs to stand out as such. If you label everything as urgent, people will start to resent or ignore the warning. If something can't wait, consider a phone call instead.

In most mailers, you can also assign a priority when you read mail, to mark messages you want to remember to get back to.

CHAPTER 4

What you need to know to be productive

What you need to know to organize saved mail

Mail is a flood of messages, some of which you save.

Each week, you could get hundreds of messages. For each message, you decide to read it, print it, delete it, save it as a file, or keep it as a message. Even if you only save a few mail messages a day, over time they mount up.

Keeping the mail messages that you want to save (and finding those messages again!) is what this chapter is about.

You can save messages as messages, either in your inbox or in mail folders.

The advantage of saving a message *as* a message is that you keep the header information. Then you can access the messages with a program that takes advantage of the header information. You can scan a list of message summaries and see the context of date sent, sender, message size, and a multiword subject. You can sort by subject or date. You can search through files for a word or phrase.

Mailers generally let you both preserve messages in the inbox and save messages in other folders that you can read while in the mail program.

How do you deal with messages that you want to save?

I don't save mail to folders. I read things and act on them. I print what I want to save or refer to.

That method works for me, since I'm on the road a lot of the time.

My biggest problem in dealing with mail is the question, "Do I need to save this?" You never know what you'll end up wanting. Then you get too many files or too many papers to keep track of.

Hugh Brown

Where mail is stored before you read it with your mailer

Incoming mail is stored in a file

Incoming mail does not come directly to your mail program. Incoming mail (as well as mail that has not yet been deleted or saved) is stored in a file on your terminal's server or network.

How mail messages are stored—before you access them with your mail program—varies by system and site:

- Many systems store all incoming messages for a single address in a single text file. When a new message comes in, it is appended to the appropriate user's text file.

- A few systems store each incoming message in a separate file. As new messages come in, new files are created.

- When a message comes in addressed to more than one user at the site, a system might either store separate messages for each user, or it might store a single copy of the message, along with a pointer to the stored message for each user.

When you start the mail program, the mailer looks for the file(s) that correspond to your incoming mail. The mailer reads the file(s), searches for the header that begins each message, and displays the list of messages.

On some systems, the storage of messages is transparent

The incoming messages for all users are generally stored in a systemwide directory. On some systems, you can go to this directory and look at your mail as one long text file.

For example, on UNIX systems, the text files containing incoming messages are usually located in either the directory /usr/spool/mail or in /usr/mail.

You can go to such a directory and see the mail files listed for each user:

```
% cd /usr/spool/mail
% ls
allen      debbie     laura
arsenio    dick       mike
awilda     eloisa     mj
barbara    florence   ront
brian      greg       susan
carol      hugh       tomas
cathy      jonie      vee
```

On UNIX, users have "file permission" to look at the mail that is in their own mail file. For example, if I log on as laura, and give laura's password, the operating system will show me laura's mail, either when I start a mail program, or if I display the file /usr/spool/mail/laura.

If you look at your own mail file, you see all the same mail messages that you would see if you started a mail program, in one long text file:

```
more /usr/spool/mail/laura
```

If you are on a UNIX system, take a look at your incoming mail file with the more command. Knowing where things come from helps demystify them.

The inbox is for active messages, not for long-term storage.

You don't want to save huge numbers of mail messages in your incoming mailbox. There are limits to the number of incoming messages you can have—limits set by the system administrator at your site, by your mailer, and by the number of messages that you can keep track of.

System administrators can impose limits on the space that you have in your inbox. Incoming mail takes up system resources. Administrators might need messages to quickly pass from a systemwide queue into your own account, whether for performance issues or for billing purposes.

Mail programs themselves have cut-off points of how many messages they allow you to have in your inbox. For example, Mush allows 999 messages. Eudora warns you when you are running low on memory for the entire application and asks you to either clean up In/Out mailboxes or to allot more memory.

Large numbers of messages in your incoming mail can slow down the responsiveness of your mail program. For example, if you have 300 messages in the inbox, it will take longer for your mail program to open and to perform sorts, than it would if you had three messages.

If you're not close to the limits imposed by your system administrator or mailer, and even if you're not having performance problems, a very long list of messages in your inbox can still feel like a burden. Even with the ability to sort by message headers or mark messages by priority, hundreds of "current" messages are too many to comfortably manage. If you have 363 messages, how do you know what's buried back in message 24?

Most mailers let you "force" a message to stay in the incoming mailbox.

As a default action, many mailers move mail out of your inbox after you have read it. They move messages that you have read and have not deleted into a folder of received mail for storage.

How do you deal with old mail?

I get about 50 messages a day, and leave very few, unanswered, overnight.

I save too much stuff. When I know that there will be more mail coming in on a project, I gather it all up. I have about 50 folders of book proposals, but I could probably get rid of 20 or 30 that are no longer current.

I also have a folder for each person who works for me. Things gather in these folders for quite a while. I never go back and get rid of it.

At this company, I suspect that every book editor has a file for each book, duplicating tremendous disk space.

Frank Willison

I've set Eudora to always copy me on every message I send out; my outbox gets huge. I have to remember to go through and file what I need in Eudora mailboxes or in files.

Edie Freedman

I save mail to text files or I delete them.

Other mail I keep in my system mailbox, and wait until I get up to about 600 messages.

At that point I delete the first 200 messages, all at one time.

The system's worked pretty well so far. If I haven't needed a message in two weeks, I can pretty safely get rid of it.

My biggest problem in organizing old mail is that my messages are so random and cover so many areas that they are hard to group.

Allen Noren

Other mailers might delete messages that you have read, unless you specifically take an action to save a message.

Regardless of the default way your mailer treats messages once you've read them—storing them or deleting them—most mailers still allow you to force a message to stay in the inbox when you need it to. For example, you might want to keep a message that you have already read with your "current" mail, to remind yourself to take care of it.

Mailers give you different ways to force messages to stay in the inbox. For example, Elm asks you when you quit the program if you want to save read messages

Save read messages into Received folder?

By default, Mush moves read messages into a folder called mbox. However, you can keep individual messages in the inbox with the preserve command. For example, to preserve message 15 in the inbox, type:

pre 15

You can save messages to other folders or mailboxes.

A folder works the same as your mailer's inbox. A folder is a group of messages saved together with a name. Instead of the name "inbox" or "In" or "system folder," a folder has a name that you give it. A mailer can display a folder or the inbox as a list of messages.

The difference between a folder and the inbox is that you control the folder, and the mail program controls the inbox.·

- You name a folder and can delete it. The location of the inbox file is "named" by the mail program and can't be deleted by you. (Some email programs let you choose the location of your inbox, whether on a remote computer/mail server or on your local computer.)

- Messages come into a folder when you transfer messages from the inbox or another folder. Messages come into the inbox when the mail program checks with the server for messages that have come into the server addressed to your email address.

The organization of the folders is up to you.

Some mailers have default folders or mailboxes for received mail, with names like mbox or Received. You can use a single folder for all old mail, or you can create more folders.

When you create folders, you select the folder names and organization. Some people save mail into folders named for the person who sent it. Some people save mail to folders named for current projects. Some people save mail to a hierarchy of folders and subfolders that reflect how they see their entire job.

The naming of folders is up to you.

You can name a folder any filename that your system recognizes as legal. Follow the rules for length, spaces, and symbols that apply to your environment.

For example, for UNIX mailers, you need to give folders a legal UNIX filename. In general, that means letters, digits, and underscores (_). Don't use spaces or other symbols in the name (unless you already understand UNIX wildcards and special characters).

In a graphical mailer, you tell the mailer that you are naming a folder (rather than a file) by your menu selection. For example, in Eudora, you select Mailboxes and then type the name.

In a command-line mailer, you tell the mailer that you are naming a folder (rather than a file) with a symbol. For example, for Mush or command-line Z-Mail, you precede a folder name with a plus sign (+). For example, to open a folder called recipes, you would use the command:

```
folder +recipes
```

Save a message to a folder with a save command.

To save a message to a folder, you indicate the message (or group of messages), give a save command, and indicate the name of the folder.

While I'm away, the messages build up to a big backlog.

The problem is keeping up, if the list is big. What's in the first 100 messages?

I had the backlog down to 50, then I went to Interop; now the backlog is at 150.

Out of that backlog, some messages are stale. As they age, they lose their urgency. I'll probably end up saving 3 or 4.

Tim O'Reilly

Using folders with sample mailers

Pine

Folders are kept in a directory called mail in your home directory. By default, saved messages are saved to a folder called saved_messages.

To save a message to a folder, highlight the message and type s. You will see the following message:

> Folder to save message in ["saved_messages"] :

If you want the message to be saved in the default folder, press Return. If you want the message to be saved to another folder, either press the keystroke combination CTRL-T to see the list of your folders or type the name of the folder.

> Folder to save message in ["saved_messages"] : sales

To change to another folder, type G, for the Go to Folder command. This closes the current folder and opens another one. Pine sometimes lists a default folder to go to:

> Folder to open [inbox] :

Press Return to go to the default folder; press CTRL-T to see the list of your folders, or type the name of the folder.

Mush or command-line Z-Mail

Folder names begin with a plus sign (+), to distinguish them from filenames. To save message 12 to your +sales folder, type:

> s 12 +sales

+sales can be the name of an existing folder or a new folder that you are creating.

There is nothing magic about the + sign. It is just shorthand for the full pathname that the mail program will search for this file in the future (e.g., /home/lamb/Mail/sales). You could also save an email message with the command:

> save 12 /home/lamb/Mail/sales

(If you don't understand pathnames, check out a UNIX tutorial book such as *Learning the UNIX Operating System* from O'Reilly & Associates.)

List your existing folders with the folders command:

> folders

Change to another folder and see the messages you have saved with the folder command. For example, to change to the +sales folder:

> folder +sales

To return to your incoming mail folder:

> folder %

To delete a folder in Mush, change to that folder and delete all messages. In Z-Mail, give the rmfolder command followed by the folder name:

> rmfolder +sales

Eudora for the Macintosh

Eudora stores messages in mailboxes. You can also group mailboxes together into folders.

You can move messages to a mailbox. Select Transfer and choose either a new or existing mailbox.

You can perform various functions on mailboxes in the Mailboxes menu. Select Special and choose Mailboxes. The options are:

- To see the messages in a folder, double-click on the folder name.
- To rename a mailbox, highlight the mailbox, select Rename, and type in the new name.
- To remove a mailbox, highlight the mailbox and select Remove.
- To create a mailbox or folder of mailboxes, select New, type in the name, select whether that name is to be a mailbox (where you can store messages) or a folder (where you organize mailboxes together).

What you need to know to organize saved mail

For example, in cc:Mail, highlight a message, select the Store SmartIcon, choose Move and Folder, and type the name of the folder.

In Mush, the command

```
s 12 +personal
```

saves message 12 to a folder called +personal.

Show a list of folders.

You can give a command to list your existing folders. In Eudora, select either Mailboxes or Transfer to see the list of mailboxes. You can elect to sort the mailboxes alphabetically or by date last accessed.

In Mush, the command:

```
folders
```

shows you the list of existing folders.

Read the mail saved to a folder by opening that folder.

Once you've saved messages in a folder, how can you see them again? Do it by changing your current folder with the folder command. When you change folders, any changes you've made in your current folder (like deleting messages) are performed; then your mailer shows you a list of the messages in the new folder.

In Pine, to open another mailbox, press G for the Go to Folder command, then type the name of the folder or press CTRL-T to see the list of folders.

Change message subjects or edit text for faster retrieval.

Sometimes you want to save a message, but you wish that it had another subject. For example, you might receive a message that contains a product number that you want to save, but its subject is "Stuff" or "Re: productivity." You could legitimately worry that it would take you a long time to access that information in the future, since the message is not clearly labeled with what you consider important.

How do you use folders?

I started using folders in '92, when I discovered them.

When I was corporate sales manager, I had folders for each sales campaign. For example, I had a folder for PEXlib and a folder for online books. For each sales folder, I would then have 25 or so subfolders, by company name.

I also had folders for the editorial development that I did with the corporations. Under an overall DCE folder [Distributed Computing Environment], I have 20 or 25 subfolders: DCE.prices, DCE.promos, DCE.leads, DCE.reviewers. If I would have a lot of mail about DCE with one company, I would give that company its own subfolder.

It got to be too complicated. I need to delete some folders.

Linda Walsh

You might also want to save a message in edited form. For example, you might receive a 400-line message with a 10-line paragraph in the middle somewhere that you need to save. If you don't want to have to wade through all 400 lines each time you look up the information, you'll want to delete the lines that will get in your way.

Some mailers let you edit messages. For example, in Mush, the command

```
e 12
```

puts the content of an email message into a text editor for you to edit. You can edit any of the fields in the header, such as the Subject, or you can delete or add text to the body. After you finish editing the message, you can save it to a folder in the normal way, e.g.:

```
s 12 +sales
```

If your mailer won't let you edit a message, you can still save a message with a corrected Subject: or amended text. Start a message to yourself, read in the message that you want to save, and mail the message to yourself.

On occasion, clean out old messages and folders.

You probably won't be able to set up one organization of folders that will work for all time. Your job responsibilities/company/interests/friends/projects can change. Folders tend to proliferate over time. (Some people who have been using folders for years might have 100+ folders.)

You'll need to do some cleaning up when you get folders that:

- Are so numerous, you can't easily scan them all on a list.

- Have titles that are complete mysteries to you.

- Don't match your current mental map of how you see yourself or your job.

Cleaning up folders is largely a matter of deletion. For example, in Eudora choose Mailboxes from the Special menu; highlight the mailbox and choose Remove. In Mush, go into a folder, delete all messages with the command:

```
d *
```

and then leave the folder.

Using "date modified" to houseclean

One way to think about cleaning out folders is by the date you last used them. If you have 200 folders, many of which are out of date, you can find the date on which all folders were last modified and delete those folders older than a year. (The date that a folder was last modified is the last time that you saved a message to that folder or made any other change.)

Some mailers let you list folders or mailboxes by date. For example, with Eudora, display the Mail directory to see the list of mailboxes and then select Display by date. From that sorted list of mailboxes, you can easily see which mailboxes have not been modified for a long time and can make deletions.

If you have hundreds of folders in a UNIX mailer, you can be creative with sorting. Remembering that folders are really just files, you can go to the directory where your folders are stored:

    cd ~/Mail

(Look in your .mailrc or other "dot-rc" file if you aren't sure of the directory name.)

Once in your mail directory, you can list the files (folders) by date. If you aren't familiar with the options for the list command, check them with the man command:

    man ls

You can list files by date order. On the system at our site, the command ls −lt lists files in long format, in chronological order:

    % ls −lt
    -rw------- 1 jack   5000 Apr 19 1994 401K
    -rw------- 1 jack   14816 May 5 1994 tech
    -rw------- 1 jack   73680 May 8 1994 personal
    -rw------- 1 jack   81549 Jul 13 09:39 questionnaire
    -rw------- 1 jack   162864 Aug 9 08:57 tradeshows
    -rw------- 1 jack   6599 Oct 12 09:00 sigs
    -rw------- 1 jack   169184 Oct 21 11:32 sales.figs
    -rw------- 1 jack   871071 Nov 9 09:11 sales.notes
    -rw------- 1 jack   15235 Nov 28 16:03 travel
    -rw------- 1 jack   82110 Dec 7 10:02 laptop

If you look at folders in chronological order, it is easier to pick out the folders that you don't want to save anymore.

How do you organize old mail?

I have mailboxes for:

- *Current projects*
- *Employment (for info on our 401K plan, etc.)*
- *Personal*
- *Events*
- *Photoshop tips, from when I subscribed to the Photoshop Club mailing list.*
- *General information about company products.*

I view the mailboxes by date, so that the most active folders are at the top.

Ted Meister

You might also want to consolidate folders. For example, you might have saved a number of messages to a folder called sales.notes. Through forgetfulness or mistyping, you might save some messages to sales.note (missing the final "s"). You'll want to have all similar messages in one folder, so that you can access them together. Go to the misnamed folder and move all the messages to the correctly-named folder.

Even if you keep a folder, you might still want to delete some of the messages in that folder. You can use the same commands to sort, pick, and delete that are described in Chapter 3. Keep only the messages that you really want; that way, you'll conserve time in opening folders and searching through messages, and you'll conserve file space.

What you need to know to organize saved mail

CHAPTER 5

What you need to know to send mail over networks

You can send email anywhere in the world.

Being able to send mail over networks means that you can send mail to any user with an email account. You can freely and quickly access millions of people and nearly unlimited information.

However, sending mail across networks can also be confusing. Address formats can vary; bounced mail messages can look formidable.

This chapter is meant to give you enough background about addressing mail so that you can venture more confidently beyond your own computer system.

Email is very reliable, as long as the address is right.

Email sometimes fails because machines or pieces of the network are unavailable. However, computers on the network are usually set up to keep trying to send mail for days before giving up, and most temporary network problems are overcome. Whether or not your email gets to its destination depends almost solely on whether or not the address is constructed correctly.

I had to learn why mail bounces

I am now the "listmaster" of our company list processor. I get all the error messages that come back after we send out email announcements to our address lists.

When I started the job, I had to learn why mail bounced. I had to learn which mail had already gone through, even though it generated an error message. I had to learn which problems were temporary, and which problems were permanent and needed to be dealt with.

Stephanie Davis

Finding an address

Why might your mail not be addressed correctly?

- You could make a typing mistake.
- You could be given an incorrect or incomplete address, if the person giving the address doesn't know much about email.
- You could be given an ambiguous-looking address. For example, you might get a handwritten address or a blurred fax and have to guess at what it really says.
- You could be given an address from a different network that needs to be "translated" into a format that your mailer and network will understand.

There is no email "phone directory" that covers every email user.

Even if you could find a directory that listed everyone's email address, the directory would:

- Be in constant flux as users change location and work responsibilities.
- Have to cover many different possible formats.
- Cause worries about security and privacy.
- Be unable to tell you if a person with a mailbox actually read mail often (or if the mailbox contained only old, unread messages).
- Be unable to tell you which address a person with multiple addresses commonly uses.

The best way to find someone's email address—and to find out whether they actually read email—is to pick up the phone, write a (paper) letter, or send a fax.

Some people don't know their "network address," the address for people to use from outside their companies. So compare the address they give you to what you learn in this chapter about addressing conventions. If the address doesn't look like one you can use, ask the person if they're sure the address will work across the network.

Different networks use a variety of address styles.

When a message comes to you, the address shown on the From: line is in a format determined by your mail system. Mail systems try to change addresses to formats that they recognize and can work with.

Your system probably uses one of the following styles of email addresses:

Internet address	*Kate@nws.baug.BG*
UUCP address	*uunet!chem.ysr.edu!richp*
DECNET address	*CHEM::RICHP*
CompuServe address	*76543,123*
Sprintmail address	*RICHP/YOYODYNE/TELEMAIL/US*
Bitnet address	*rich@yoyodyne.bitnet*

Many people send mail only within their own network, especially if they are on a very large network such as the Internet. But understanding other address formats will help you to avoid easy addressing mistakes, to do your own troubleshooting when you get a message "bounced" as undeliverable, and to venture sending mail to another network when the addressing is not quite the same as your own.

We'll start with Internet-style addresses, since the Internet is the network with the largest number of users.

Internet addresses have two parts: the who and the where.

Internet addresses are written in two parts: who the message is to and where the computer is located, separated by an at-sign (@). For example:

ronp@chem.ysr.edu

In this case, *ronp* is the recipient, and *chem.ysr.edu* is the computer location.

Within your company, you might be able to send mail to simpler, local addresses as a convenience. You might be able to

The "finger" command on UNIX systems

The finger command lets you find out someone's login name (hence the email address) if you know what computer your correspondent uses.

For example, if you were looking for Frank Willison's email address and knew that he uses a computer called *roa.com*, you could give the command:

finger Frank@roa.com

You would get back information on all users whose first or last name matches "Frank" or who have chosen "Frank" as their login ID. Remember that UNIX is case-sensitive.

Finger only works if a system is directly on the Internet. Also, many systems disable finger for security reasons.

send mail to other people in your company by typing only their login names, e.g.:

```
mail frank,carol
```

Behind the scene, the computer does the work of expanding the local addresses into the full addresses (*frank@roa.com* and *carol@rock.west.roa.com*) needed for delivery.

Even if you can send mail to a person within your company by knowing only his login name, that person still has a full email address. Whenever you send email across a network, you have to supply the entire address, including the location's computer name.

The first part of an Internet address, "who," can be a person's name, a group alias, or a mailbox for a function.

The "who" of the address is most often a single user. Some companies or organizations have conventions for the format of a user name. Depending on the conventions of the system, my user name might be:

```
Linda.Lamb
Linda_Lamb
llamb
lamb
lindal
```

Some organizations use computer account numbers as mailbox names. In that case, a user name could be something cryptic, such as *xy123AB*.

The "who" of the address can also be a group of users. For example, mail sent to the alias "marketing" might be routed to ten different people who belong to that group.

The "who" of an address can also be the place to put mail for a function. The following naming conventions are used for Internet mailboxes:

x-users

> Mailbox names with dashes in them often signify a group use, such as a distribution list or mailing list to a group of people.

bluebirds-request
> Mailbox names ending in -request are administrative addresses for distribution lists. This kind of address is where to send requests to subscribe or unsubscribe to a mailing list.

postmaster
> Every site is supposed to have a postmaster mailbox (postman or postmast in BITNET) to which you can address questions and report problems concerning the mail system.

mailer-daemon
> This address is the name of a UNIX mail system program. Messages coming from such an address are most likely reporting problems with delivery of your mail message.

The "who" part can contain comments that are passed on, but are otherwise ignored by the mailer.

When you see a sender's address in the From: field of your message, the address may contain a comment, such as the sender's name. For example, here are three ways that an address might appear:

```
From: kate@nws.baug.bg
From: kate@nws.baug.bg (Katherine Sundgren)
From: Katherine Sundgren <kate@nws.baug.bg>
```

Comments can be put in parentheses ( ), as in the second address, or angle brackets < >, as in the third address. The mail system treats all three addresses identically, because it only looks at the mail address, *kate@nws.baug.bg*.

The second part of an Internet address, "where," is the computer's location.

The part of the address to the right of the @ is the location of the computer, or the *domain* name. The domain is split into subdomains, separated by periods.

The rightmost part is the first-level domain. For example, in the address *joan@roa.com, com* is the first-level domain. This first-level domain can indicate the type of site, such as:

Sample Australian subdomains

Andersen Consulting: *andersen.com.au*

Apple Computer Australia Pty. Ltd: *apple.oz.au*

Australian Public Access Network Association: *apana.org.au*

Australian Sports Commission: *ausport.gov.au*

Division of Information Technology: *csis.dit.csiro.au*

Division of Wildlife and Ecology: *dwe.csiro.au*

Emergent Technology: *emergent.com.au*

Queensland University of Technology: *qut.edu.au*

South Australian Department of Roads: *roads.sa.gov.au*

Wesley College: *wesley.oz.au*

edu	educational
com	commercial
org	nonprofit organization
net	networking organization
gov	government installation
mil	military installation

Or, the first-level domain can be a two-letter country code. In the address *kate@nws.baug.bg*, *bg* is the top-level domain, which stands for Bulgaria.

Second-level domains can be company names, university names, organization names, city names, etc.

Knowing these addressing conventions, you can tell if an Internet address "looks right."

As you become familiar with first-level and second-level domains, you can begin to make sense of the addresses that you see on the Internet. For example, an address of:

ronp@chem.ysr.edu

looks as if it is for someone named Ron who works in the Chemistry department at a university.

postmaster@eiunet.ie

is the address of the postmaster at a site in Ireland.

You can translate the address of another network into an Internet-style address.

If you send mail using Internet-style addresses, how do you send mail when the address is from a different network and in a different format?

For most networks, you can add an Internet-style suffix to the user's address on his network. For other mail gateways, the conversion of an address to an Internet-style address is more complicated. The sidebars "Translating addresses to Internet style" and "Converting various other networks' addresses to

Internet-style addresses" show conversion instructions for addresses of various networks.

The mail system sends you a message if delivery is delayed.

If your mail is taking longer than expected to deliver, but the mail system hasn't given up trying, you will probably get an email message warning you of the delay. The message will identify the sender as "mailer-daemon."

Why might there be a delay in delivery? One reason might be that the host computer that you're trying to reach is having temporary network difficulties (e.g., a power outage).

Warning messages usually say something like "Message not delivered in four hours; still trying." For example:

```
Subject: Undeliverable Mail
Attempting to deliver following mail to recipient(s):
<winter@piazza.iaea.or.at>
IAEA1.IAEA.OR.AT unable to connect for 1 days to recipient
host.
Delivery will be attempted for a total of 7 days.
** Text of Mail follows **
```

The Subject: in this sample message, "Undeliverable Mail," doesn't necessarily mean that the mail will never be deliverable. The body of the warning message shows the address that the computer is trying to reach, the name of the computer that's trying to do the delivery, the problem "unable to connect for 1 days to recipient host," and how long it'll keep trying (7 days). The end of the warning message includes a copy of the original message header and body, for your reference.

When you get a warning, don't resend the original message— because your new message will wait, too. If your original message was urgent, you might try a phone call instead.

The mail system bounces mail back to you if the mail is undeliverable, along with some explanation of why.

A message that is bounced won't be delivered. A sample bounce message might read:

Japanese Subdomains

AI Language Research Institute, Ltd.: *air.co.jp*

Aichi University of Education: *aichi-edu.ac.jp*

Anritsu Corp.: *anritsu.co.jp*

Communication Net Corporation: *comm-net.co.jp*

Information Processing Society of Japan: *ipsj.or.jp*

Kochi University: *kochi-u.ac.jp*

Nagasaki Prefectural Government: *nagasaki.go.jp*

NHK (Japan Broadcasting Corporation): *nhk.or.jp*

Oita University: *oita-u.ac.jp*

Packet Radio User's Group: *prug.or.jp*

Translating addresses to Internet style

The following table shows, for selected networks, the suffix to add to a user ID to turn it into an Internet-style address:

Network	Send mail to
Alternex	*user*@ax.apc.org
ALAnet	*user*%ALANET@intermail.isi.edu
AmericaOnline	*user*@aol.com
Applelink	*user*@applelink.com
ATTmail	*user*@attmail.com
BIX	*user*@bix.com
CGNnet	*user*%CGNET@intermail.isi.edu
Chasque	*user*@chasque.apc.org
Comlink	*user*@oln.comlink.apc.org
Delphi	*user*@delphi.com
Econet	*user*@igc.apc.org
Ecuanex	*user*@ecuanex.apc.org
eWorld	*user*@online.apple.com
Genie	*user*@genie.geis.com

GeoNet	*user*@geo1.geonet.de
	     for recipients in Europe
	user@geo2.geonet.de
	     for recipients in the UK
	user@geo4.geonet.de
	     for recipients in North America

Glasnet	*user*@glas.apc.org
Greenet	*user*@gn.apc.org
Nasamail	*user*@nasamail.nasa.gov
Nicarao	*user*@nicarao.apc.org
Niftyserve	*user*@niftyserve.or.jp
Nordnet	*user*@pns.apc.org
Peacenet	*user*@igc.apc.org
Pegasus	*user*@peg.apc.org
Prodigy	*user*@prodigy.com alphanumeric ID rather than the user's name
Pronet	*user*@tanus.oz.au
Web	*user*@web.apc.org

Converting various other networks' addresses to Internet-style addresses

Bitnet

Bitnet addresses normally have the form *name@host.bitnet*, e.g.:

richp@yoyodyne.bitnet

To translate this address into an Internet-style address, use a user name of *name%host* and add the address of a Bitnet-Internet gateway for the machine-name side, e.g., *cunyvm.cuny.edu*. Separate the two with an at-sign (@). For example, rewrite the address above as:

richp%yoyodyne@cunyvm.cuny.edu.

Ask your system administrator or local help desk for the best gateway for you to use.

CompuServe

CompuServe addresses consist of two numbers separated by a comma, e.g.:

76543,123

In Internet-style addresses, a comma is interpreted as separating two addresses, so you have to change the comma to a period before adding the machine location:

76543.123@compuserve.com

Fidonet

Fidonet addresses consist of a first and last name and a set of numbers in the form *a:b/c.d*.

williemartin1:5/2.3

To make this address into an Internet-style address, you separate the first and last names by a period, and send to p*d.fc.nb.za.*fidonet.org. For example, translate the above address to:

willie.martin@p3.f2.n5.z1.fidonet.org

If your machine has trouble with that address format, you can also try sending mail directly to the gateway machine:

willie.martin%p3.f2.n5.z1.fidonet.org@zeus.ieee.org

Sprintmail

A full Sprintmail address looks like:

John Bigboote/YOYODYNE/TELEMAIL/US

Within Sprintmail, the address is abbreviated:

John Bigboote/YOYODYNE

When someone gives you a Sprintmail address, they often provide only the abbreviated version of the address. You will have to supply the full address and translate that:

/PN=John.Bigboote/O=YOYODYNE/ADMD=
TELEMAIL/C=US/@sprint.com

MCImail

MCI mailboxes have both an address and a person's name associated with them. The address looks like a telephone number, e.g., *1234567*.

A person with a mail account can give you either the address or their name. If you have the number, use the number on the left side of the @ sign:

1234567@mcimail.com

If you are given the name of a person on MCImail, you can address it with an underline separating the first and last names, e.g.:

John_Bigboote@mcimail.com

UUCP

A UUCP-style address has two possible formats. It can look like *name@host.uucp*:

john_w@yoyodyne.uucp

Or it can look like *!uunet!host!name*:

uunet!yoyodyne!john_w

If you are given such an address, you will need to provide the name of a UUCP-Internet gateway as the machine name. Ask your system administrator or help desk for the correct gateway to use. The above address might be translated:

john_w%yoyodyne@uu.psi.com

The most messages I ever saw in a queue were 1,876 to the listown address that I manage.

These messages were bad addresses that had bounced. The number of bounces was exaggerated, because we had done multiple postings that day. Also, listproc— the program we use to administer the list of names—had gone buggy and was delivering double bounce messages for every error.

Stephanie Davis

```
TWNMOE10.Edu.TW unable to deliver following mail to
recipient(s):
<aliu@ap243.ntty.edu.tw>
TWNMOE10.Edu.TW unable to connect for 3 days to recipient
host.
** Text of Mail follows **
```

This format is common. The bounced mail starts with a message header and body that explain the problem. The original message comes at the end.

Like a lot of the bounces you'll see, this message doesn't say clearly that the computer will not keep trying to deliver the mail. But you can get a good clue that the computer won't be trying any more from the words "unable to deliver" and "unable to connect for 3 days," with no mention of trying any longer.

Messages most often bounce because of an addressing error.

The most likely reason for a message to bounce is that the address is wrong: the format of the address is not correct, the target computer that you want to reach is unknown or can't be found, or the target computer does not recognize the user name that you have given.

You will also occasionally see messages bounce because of system errors. These errors are not in your control and can be quite varied and esoteric. For example:

- When a message is sent, it may take at least several hops to get to where it's going. The message may take too many hops or bounce back and forth between two computers. The mail system may not be able to deliver an error message to a human to fix the problem (e.g., if there is no postmaster address at a site).

- The target computer may be overloaded with too many processes, and a system administrator might need to take down the system and restart it.

- The target computer may refuse messages.

- Your local computer may be having trouble routing a message.

When an address is wrong, try some simple troubleshooting.

When you get a bounce message, there's no reason to panic. If you wade through the lines of the message header, you'll find some lines in plain language. Each bounce or warning that you read will give you more experience in dealing with them.

When the bounce shows an invalid address (host unknown, user unknown), you can do some basic troubleshooting and perhaps get your message through.

1) Does the address look right?

Look at the To: field and see if there are any obvious errors. Did you type the address correctly? Does the address include a machine name? Do the first-level and second-level domains make sense? Are there any spaces or stray punctuation that could be causing problems?

2) Are there differences in addresses in the From:, Reply to:, and To: headers?

Sometimes, different networks can change a header while delivering the mail. Are the From: and Reply to: fields the same? Is there an email address included in the signature at the end of the message? If you replied automatically to a message (with r or R, for example), you might try resending the message and type out the correct address found in the From: field.

3) Can you use another method of communication to contact the person?

What other methods of contact are open to you? Do you have a phone number for the person or company that you are trying to contact? Do you have a mutual acquaintance who might have an email address or phone number?

4) Ask for help

If you have a mail problem you can't solve, ask your local resources such as a help desk or system administrator.

All sites on the Internet should have an address called *postmaster*. You can send a request for help with a mail problem to that address. For example, if you're trying to send mail to Ron

On UNIX systems, use the verify command to check that the user is known

On a UNIX system, the verify program can let you check addresses for users (or groups of users or functions) at any site that allows checking of its addresses.

You can use verify to check a local address by typing verify and then the local email address:

```
% verify lamb
verifying lamb locally
Linda Lamb <lamb@rock.west.roa.com>
```

The response you get shows that the address is valid and also shows the full, expanded email address.

You can use verify to check the users listed under a local alias. For example, to see who is included in a "cs" (customer service) alias:

```
% verify cs
verifying cs locally
Ginger Clemons <ginger@rock.roa.com>
Marlene Salonga <salonga@rock.roa.com>
Carol Sholes <sholes@rock.roa.com>
Marianne Cooke <marianne@rock.roa.com>
Awilda Scott <awilda@rock.roa.com>
Marlene McBride <marlene@rock.roa.com>
Julianne Panick <julianne@rock.roa.com>
Kathi Coffey <kathi@rock.roa.com>
Greg Goben <greg@rock.roa.com>
Carol Vogt <carol@rock.roa.com>
Vee McMillen <vee@rock.roa.com>
Debbie Pichulo <debp@rock.roa.com>
```

Since aliases might be maintained on remote computers, you might need to give the full address. For example, if a sales alias exists at your company, but is maintained on another machine, the command verify sales only shows that the alias exists:

```
%verify sales
verifying sales locally
<sales@roa.com>
```

To see the people on the sales alias, you would have to give the entire address:

```
%verify sales@roa.com
```

To determine what went wrong with bounced mail, you can use verify to see if a user name is recognized at a remote site. For example, if you are trying to decipher a written email address and can't tell if the user name is jan or jane, you can question the site with verify .

```
% verify jan@roa.com
verifying jan at roa.com
jan... User unknown
% verify jane@roa.com
verifying jane at roa.com
Jane Appleyard <jane@roa.com>
```

It is possible that both user names exist at the site, but seeing the full names can give you a good chance of choosing the correct address.

verify is not included in an off-the-shelf UNIX operating system. You might not have verify on your system. To test, just type verify and any email address, such as your own. If your computer doesn't recognize the verify command, you will see an error message:

```
% verify lamb
verify: Command not found
```

You can ask your system administrator to add the verify program. The program is free and can be obtained via FTP from *shiva.com:/src/MAIL/verify*.

What you need to know to send mail over networks

Petrusha at the address *ronp@chem.ysr.edu*, you could send mail to the postmaster there:

```
mail postmaster@chem.ysr.edu
```

Be aware that the person who answers postmaster mail is usually very busy. Before mailing a request to the postmaster, make sure that your problem is a real one, that the message is critical, that you tried to answer your question locally, and that you have no other options.

The header of a message can be changed to a different format.

The header of a message is often changed, since email systems and networks have different standards for addresses.

When you send mail from one network to another network, the mail passes through a gateway computer that usually tries to convert your style of email addresses to its own standards. For example, if you're sending mail with Internet-style addresses to a person on CompuServe, your mail will go through a gateway computer that tries to translate Internet-style addresses to CompuServe-style addresses.

That conversion doesn't always work. The gateway computer might convert some of the addresses in a header but leave the rest. For example, some email systems don't have separate From: and Reply-to: fields. If you use both fields in your mail message, a gateway computer might ignore one of them.

The text of a message can also be mangled.

The message that you're sending over networks can get mangled or "munged." Some mail gateways delete white space (blanks) at the ends of lines in a message; some will add white space.

You can't know ahead of time whether or not your message will be munged. If you're sending a plain message—with no attachments or files—then you probably don't have to worry. Remember to use relatively short lines, e.g., 60 characters, and not to use tabs, to increase the chances of your mail getting through unscathed.

Check the address

Look at the address before you send mail out over the Net, to see if there are any typos.

You don't always get your mail message back. If you send mail to a valid host, but mistype the user name, a lot of times the host computer will send you back an error message, but without the message body (to "save bandwidth").

So, if you're sending something to a long, unfamiliar address, check it first before mailing and save yourself having to possibly retype the message.

Stephanie Davis

Check the address again

My fingers do get used to typing certain email addresses.

On one occasion, I thought I was sending mail to one friend, but ended up having typed the address of another friend to whom I send mail much more frequently.

Luckily, I didn't say anything I regretted.

However, that kind of experience makes me more careful in checking the To: field, especially if I'm saying anything remotely controversial.

Arsenio Santos

Asking a postmaster for help

If your mail is of great importance, and you know the site name but can't locate the user, you can send mail to postmaster at that site.

You can ask for help and tell them what you think the address should be. Polite grovelling is the appropriate tone.

If the mail is indeed important, you'll be surprised at how helpful a postmaster can be.

If the mail is frivolous, you'll be surprised at how nasty a postmaster can be.

Mary Jane
Caswell-Stephenson

If the person who gets your message complains that it looks funny, that they can't reply to it, and so on, talk to your help desk consultants.

If the body of your message is getting munged, both you and the recipient could use MIME mail as a way to work around the problem. MIME was designed to get through gateways and other mail-mungers. It's especially useful for mailing files. (See Chapter 9.)

Don't send unsolicited, commercial, or broadcast messages.

Computer networks give users the power to quickly reach many people. However, people on the network usually expect to receive only appropriate mail in their mailboxes. They expect communications from colleagues or from groups that they have subscribed to for specific purposes.

If you do broadcast a message to many people, make sure that you know where it's going and that the list of addresses to which you're sending it is appropriate for that purpose. For example, don't send messages to mailing lists unless you're sure that the list allows, or even encourages, the kind of message you want to send.

If you do broadcast a message inappropriately, some people may send you angry replies—or, in extreme cases, send mail to your manager or postmaster to ask that your account be cancelled for abusing your email privileges.

Some users pay fees for receiving your mail.

Sending mail within many local systems is virtually free and unlimited. But when your mail goes onto a network, especially an international network, someone may have to pay fees. If you're sending large or frequent messages to someone you don't know, you might check first whether they'll have to pay to receive your mail.

Networks in some developing countries may not have much capacity. You should be careful not to send large messages—more than a few thousand characters—unless you first ask the recipient (or the recipient's postmaster).

Resources

- The book *!%@:: A Directory of Electronic Mail Addressing and Networks* (O'Reilly & Associates) lists country codes, subdomains, and the format of email addresses to reach over 180 major networks (among other information).

- There is an online guide to finding people's email addresses. It first recommends direct contact (like making a few phone calls), but then describes other things you can dabble with, like email address policies at colleges and universities, using the Inter_Network Mail Guide, the whois database, etc. This guide is written as a FAQ posting. If you have a WWW browser, use the URL:

  ```
  http://www/cis.ohio-state.edu/hypertext/faq/usenet/
  finding-addresses/faq.html
  ```

  If you can read Usenet newsgroups, look in *news.answers* for the FAQ.

- *The Whole Internet User's Guide and Catalog* (O'Reilly & Associates) talks more about Internet addressing. *The Whole Internet* also contains a catalog of Internet locations and addresses where you can look up information. A free online version of the Whole Internet Catalog also exists. If you have a WWW browser, open the URL:

  ```
  http://gnn.com/gnn/wic/index.html
  ```

Remember who's on the other end of the line

I work at a company with an Internet connection and X workstations. I try to remember that not everyone has such a fast, inexpensive connection.

Some people have to pay, personally, for their Internet connection. Some people have to pay by the message, by the size of the message, or by connect time.

I try to imagine that the other person is the Professor on a Gilligan's Island computer that is put together with coconuts.

Arsenio Santos

I imagine my readers on a VT52 terminal and a 2400 baud connection. That helps me keep my messages brief.

Mary Jane Caswell-Stephenson

CHAPTER 6

What you need to know about mailing lists

The mechanics of subscribing to a mailing list can be mystifying.

Mailing lists can expand your circle of colleagues and add depth to an interest. Many people don't subscribe to any lists, however—either because they don't know about lists or because they don't have time to deal with the number of mail messages that a list generates. Most people who *do* subscribe only subscribe to one or two lists.

It is precisely because people subscribe so infrequently that errors are made. People subscribe to the wrong address and get *flamed* with nasty email responses. Perfectly nice, intelligent people are afraid to unsubscribe because they can't find an address.

This chapter takes the mystery and trepidation out of something you'll do infrequently—finding and joining a new mailing list.

A mailing list is like a group discussion.

A mailing list is a group of addressees who can all be reached by sending an email message to a single address. A mailing list can be:

What mailing lists do you recommend?

LA Lakers: a sports discussion about the Los Angeles Lakers, a US basketball team.

Hugh Brown

Animal Rights Activism, an animal rights list that talks about issues, legislative alerts, and demonstrations.

Olivia Bogdan

- A place to exchange ideas
- A way to access other people in the world who share common interests
- A support group, a sounding board, or a guide

For example, suppose that a historian studying 19th-century life has subscribed to the mailing list called *century19*. If she has a question, she might start her email program and send a message to the mailing list:

```
From: js@history.yu.edu (Jill Smoots)
To: century19@yu.edu
Subject: Victorian table manners

Have any of you seen bibliographies or other references to
etiquette at Victorian-era meals? Thanks.
```

Jill's message will go to the address *century19*. That address was created by a computer administrator as an alias for a mailing list. Jill's message will go to each person who has subscribed to the *century19* mailing list—whether that list is tens or thousands of other people. These subscribers will see Jill's message the next time they read email, mixed in with their mail from other people, and possibly mail from other mailing lists.

Another *century19* subscriber in Manchester (U.K.) sees Jill's message. Like Jill, he sends his message to the *century19* address:

```
From: frank@pu.ac.uk (F. Church)
To: century19@yu.edu
Subject: Re: Victorian table manners

I heard a fascinating paper on that subject at a conference
a few years ago. I can't find a citation, though. The
conference was in New York, I believe, and the paper was by
a doctoral candidate from Harvard.
```

Frank's message goes to everyone on the list. It feeds the discussion that Jill started. Another person on the list knows the author of the paper that Frank mentioned, so she mails that information to the list. Three other people who want to know more about the subject send private messages to Jill, asking for a summary of what she finds out.

Soon, Jill has her answers—and these colleagues have wrapped up another discussion on the mailing list.

To join a mailing list, you need to be on a computer that connects to a computer network.

There are hundreds of mailing lists "out there."

If your computer is connected to the Internet, you can join virtually any mailing list. You can subscribe to lists on the Internet as well as to lists on other networks that are connected to the Internet.

Your network might not have gateways to other networks. If not, ask other users or your system's postmaster if there are any mailing lists (also called discussion groups, Listservs, or roundtables) available on your local system. When computers are shared by a department or company, you don't need a network to have email discussions with your colleagues.

Find lists by asking your coworkers or looking at online sources.

Where do you start looking for mailing lists of interest?

Ask your coworkers. If you work in a educational, library, medical, business, or computer environment that has Internet access, there is probably a coworker who is subscribing to a mailing list in which you would be interested.

You can also look up mailing lists online. There are a few lists of all mailing lists. And there are some edited lists of mailing lists, highlighting only those the editor feels are most worthwhile. The Resources section at the end of this chapter has some addresses where you can check for mailing lists.

Mailing lists are administered by a person, with help from a program.

There is at least one person involved with each list. That person—the list owner—starts the list and keeps it going. The person who is the list owner is often a volunteer, doing the work because they are interested in the subject.

If the list is small, sometimes the list owner does all the administration by hand: adding and deleting subscribers, forwarding messages to the list subscribers, answering questions.

Using a mailing list for support

I had an overuse injury to my thumbs that restricted my activities at work and home. One of the things that I did was to subscribe to the mailing group Sorehand.

Sorehand (its subscribers and its archives) told me about stress-free postures and taking work breaks; recommended books, physicians, clinics, and body awareness classes; talked about how driving aggravates the condition and what to do about it; summarized information on ergonomic keyboards and kitchen tools; commiserated with pain.

It's great to talk to someone else who's already "been there."

Linda Lamb

However, most list owners use computer programs to help with routing and the daily administration load. Computer programs are available all day, every day, and can handle hundreds or thousands of subscribers.

Three of the programs most often used to administer mailing lists are Majordomo, Listproc, and Listserv.

Even if a list owner uses a program for most daily administrative tasks, he or she still has to take over when the program can't resolve a problem: to handle complaints, to resolve what to do with mail that is undeliverable, and to write the "automatic" replies that the mailing list program sends out.

Some list owners take on the additional work of "moderating" their list, to save subscribers from receiving inappropriate messages. The moderator screens all messages that come in to the broadcast address before sending them on to all other subscribers.

A list moderator filters out inappropriate administrative messages, such as subscribe or unsubscribe messages, and answers those messages personally. A list moderator also filters out other inappropriate messages, such as messages that should be sent privately rather than broadcast to the whole group or commercial messages that shouldn't be posted at all.

Every mailing list has two addresses: a broadcast address and a subscription address.

The broadcast address is the address that you use to communicate with all other subscribers on the list. You should only send mail to the broadcast address that you want everyone on the list to receive.

The subscription address for the mailing list is the address that you use for private administrative issues relating to the list.

Mailing list faux pas most often include misusing the broadcast address, such as:

- Sending a SUBSCRIBE or UNSUBSCRIBE request to the group of subscribers, rather than to the subscription address

- Sending a posting to the whole group when a private posting to one subscriber is more appropriate

- Not including your full email address (so that people can reply to you privately)

Send mail to the broadcast address when you want to broadcast to all subscribers.

When you send a message to the broadcast address, that message will be sent on to the dozens, or hundreds, or thousands of other people who subscribe to the list.

Any message that you send to the broadcast address will get broadcast. If I send the message "subscribe SOREHAND Linda Lamb" to the broadcast address, the *hundreds of subscribers* to *Sorehand* will each see that message in their personal inboxes. If you subscribe to an unmoderated mailing list, sooner or later you'll see someone make such a mistake. When you do see this, be kind and help them learn how to handle such requests.

A small percentage of lists are moderated. But you should assume that you are the only one responsible for whatever message you send to the broadcast address.

Send only administrative messages to the subscription address.

If you send a message to a subscription address in the correct format, the administrator or mailing list program can:

- Subscribe you to the mailing list
- Send you a "help" message that more fully describes the program's capabilities, addresses for archives, etc. (Most often, this help message is "canned" and very thorough.)
- Unsubscribe you from the mailing list

How you write the subscription message depends on who is reading it: a person, Listserv, Listproc, Majordomo, or another mailing list program.

When you send a message to a mailing list program, the format has to be exact. If you vary from the prescribed formula and include, for example, a greeting or a signature, the mailing list program will not know how to interpret the variation.

If your subscription message is not in the format that the mailing list program needs, it could:

- Send you a canned message to let you know what lines of your message it doesn't understand.

- Send an error message to the human who owns the list.

The subscription address tells you to whom (or what) you are speaking.

When you subscribe, you communicate either with the person who manages the mailing list, or with the program that the person has set up to deal with subscriptions. You can often tell if you're sending mail to a person or a program by the subscription address.

If you're sending a subscription to an address like one of these:

```
listproc@widget.com
LISTSERV@huntingdon.edu
Majordomo@gocart.com
```

you're dealing with one of the three major mailing list programs: Listproc, Listserv, or Majordomo. There are other mail/archive programs, such as Almanac, but these three programs are the ones that you'll probably come across most often.

Any time that you see an email address that doesn't begin with one of these program names, you should assume that you are sending mail to a person.

```
bluebirds-request@widget.com
greg.g@compsci.marly.edu
```

In addresses for mailing list subscriptions, list owners or administrators often use the suffix *-request* for an alias to collect subscription requests. For example, *bluebirds-request* could be an address answered by a person, set up for the purpose of getting subscription requests for the mailing list *bluebirds*.

(One reason that a list owner uses an alias to collect mailing list subscriptions is to separate mail as it comes in. If you were getting 50 requests a day for one kind of information, you might want to keep those requests separate from the rest of your mail. Another reason to use an alias is that it is easy for another person to take over reading that mailing list—temporarily or permanently. List administration can change behind the scenes without inconveniencing anyone in the "outside" world.)

You do not want to use a broadcast address to subscribe to—or unsubscribe from—a mailing list. You'll irritate people. Sometimes you'll irritate many people. Some of them will probably let you know they are irritated.

If you have only a broadcast address, you need to do some more investigation: go back to your source and find the subscription address. Go back to the person who gave you the suggestion for the mailing list, or back to the Usenet newsgroup, book, or mail message where you saw the reference.

You subscribe to a mailing list by sending an email message.

To subscribe to a list—so that you'll start to receive messages from it—you need to send a mail message to the subscription address. The sidebar "Steps to subscribe or unsubscribe from a list" shows procedures for subscribing and unsubscribing.

Not all lists are open to anyone who subscribes; the list may be private. Subscriptions might need to be approved by the list owner, moderator, or the other people on the list. If you don't know that when you send the subscription message, you should get a reply that asks for additional information.

Make sure that you copy yourself on mail to the subscription address, so that you'll have a record to refer to later.

Mail digests are available for some mailing lists.

Most mailing lists send out individual messages—whenever anyone sends a message to the broadcast address, that message is sent out to list members. If you're on a mailing list that sends lots of messages—especially if you don't need to get involved with discussions as soon as they happen—those individual messages can clutter your mailbox. It is a real commitment of your time to get 10, or 30, separate messages from a mailing list each day.

Instead of individual messages, you might want to receive a list digest.

Unsubscribing

Lists can be dangerous things. The documentation is all word of mouth. People don't remember how to undo what they've done.

For example, I'm on the CNI Modernization mailing list. [A discussion of Internet commercialization.] I found out about it from a coworker, and fired off a subscription message—but didn't keep a copy.

I got a lot out of the list when I was working in that area. In my present job, I don't need the info any longer.

But I haven't taken myself off the list. I don't remember how, and I'm afraid that I'm going to offend people on the list by sending mail to the wrong address.

Linda Walsh

A digest means you'll get a single mail message every so often (daily, every few days, or irregularly) instead of many separate messages spread out over that same period of time. You'll still have as much text to read, but it'll be in one piece, not in many separate pieces. If you don't have time one day to read the discussion, you'll only have to delete one digest message.

Whether you can get a digest depends on the mailing list program that runs the list. The Listserv and Listproc programs make it easy for the list owner to set up digests.

With Majordomo or by hand, digests may not be as easy. Some Majordomo sites set up duplicate lists that send digests. For example, if you subscribe to the *mud-wrestlers* list, you'll get individual messages; but by subscribing to *mud-wrestlers-digest* you will get digests of the same messages.

Check the confirmation message you get when you subscribe to a list for information about digests.

You've subscribed and you're ready to talk? Wait a while.

You may have subscribed to a list so that you can get involved. But rather than sending messages to the list right away, most people suggest waiting a while and listening instead.

You're joining a conversation already in progress. Listen for a while to what other people are saying. See what kind of group you find yourself in. Get a feel for the "style" of the list (if there is one). Are people restrained and do they post carefully-thought-out messages, or is the discussion more like "anything goes"?

People on the list may already be discussing just the thing you want to say (that happens a lot!) or might have discussed it recently.

The list could be quiet; you might not get any messages at all. If you didn't get a message to confirm your subscription, mail the list owner or moderator after a week or so to be sure that you're on the list.

There could be an FAQ that will answer your question. Ignoring the FAQ won't make you popular with other people on the list.

What you need to know about mailing lists

Where can you find out about an FAQ? Carefully read any welcome message that you received when you first subscribe. Read the mailing-list postings for a while, to see if instructions are given. If you don't see any mention of an FAQ, ask the list.

Many mailing lists also have archives. The messages from the mailing list are not only sent to people on the list; they're also stored in an archive file. Other people who want to catch up on the discussion some time later can get the archive file, read through it, send email with a follow-up, and so on.

There are two ways to respond to a posting: privately and to the entire list.

In general, there are two different places you might want to send your replies:

- Reply privately to the person who sent the original message when your reply wouldn't interest other people on the list. For instance, if you want to ask a personal question, don't bother everyone on the list when you only want an answer from the original sender. When people post to the list, their email address should be in their signature or in a From: field in the header.

- Reply to everyone on the list when you have something to share with many of the people on the list: to give your opinion, ask for other peoples' opinions, or to broaden or narrow a discussion.

If you are getting mailing-list messages one at a time, you should be able to use the mail program's Reply command to send mail back either to the poster or to the entire list. If you get the messages in digest form, using Reply always responds to the whole group.

When you start a reply, check the message header and ask yourself if you want to be replying to the entire group or to only a single poster. Change the address if you need to.

Steps to subscribe or unsubscribe from a list

1. Check that you have a subscription address.

   This might be a person's email address, an alias like cent19-request, or an address beginning with *Listserv*, *Listproc*, or *Majordomo*.

2. Deactivate your automatic signature.

   Temporarily deactivate your signature before sending a subscription to a program. You can unset your signature with the same kind of command used to set it. With command-line Z-Mail, Mush, or most versions of Mail, type "unset autosign" at the prompt.

3. Then send the message to one of the address types below.

Sending a subscription to a person

Send a message with your name, company name, telephone number, and complete email address. Copy yourself on the mail and keep your copy.

If you're feeling friendly, add a note that tells how you heard about the list and why you're interested. Feel free to include your automatic signature.

Sending a subscription to Listserv

If you are sending a subscription to Listserv, leave the Subject: empty. On the first line of the message body, type:

    subscribe listname Firstname Lastname

where Firstname Lastname is your full name, such as Britt Jensen.

With Listserv, you may request messages in digest form (rather than individual messages). So if you are named Britt Jensen, and you want to subscribe to the list *bluebird* in digest form, send the message:

    subscribe bluebird Britt Jensen
    set bluebird digests

To unsubscribe, send the message "signoff *listname*." For exmple:

    signoff bluebird

Listserv will get your email address automatically-from your message header. Copy yourself on the mail and keep your copy.

Sending a subscription to Listproc

To send a subscription to Listproc, leave the Subject: empty. On the first line of the message body, type:

    subscribe listname Firstname Lastname

You may request messages in digest form. Using the example above, you would send the message:

    subscribe bluebird Britt Jensen
    set bluebird mail digest

To unsubscribe, send the message:

    unsubscribe listname

Listproc will get your email address automatically from your message header. Copy yourself on the mail and keep your copy.

Sending a subscription to Majordomo

To send a subscription to Majordomo, leave the Subject: empty. On the first line of the message body, type:

    subscribe listname

To unsubscribe from a list, send the message:

    unsubscribe listname

Majordomo will get your name and email address automatically from your message header. Copy yourself on the mail and keep your copy.

Sending a subscription to an unknown program

If you are sending a subscription to an unknown program, send the message:

    Subject: help
    help

See your own postings, by copying yourself or by setting an acknowledgment variable.

When you send a message to a mailing list, you may not get a copy back. That doesn't mean your message wasn't sent. The program that manages the list might assume that you would save a copy if you wanted one and not waste the resources to send you another. If you want to see a copy of each of your postings, include your own address in the Cc: field.

You also may be able to configure this by sending a command to the subscription address requesting a copy of each of your messages. (Most list managers refer to such copies as "acknowledgments.") To see if you can request copies automatically, check the confirmation message you got when you subscribed, or send a help command to the subscription address.

The speed of delivery to mailing list addresses depends on delays and batching.

When you send email to another person, most email systems deliver it quickly. But mail from mailing lists might be delayed up to a day or more. Some list management programs send mail in batches—sometimes late at night when the system isn't busy. If there seems to be a delay before people get your message, that might be why.

Include your full email address in messages you send to the mailing list.

You may not have any trouble getting email from colleagues and friends; when they reply to your message, your correct address is in your message header and their email program uses it automatically.

But some people on the mailing list may not be that lucky, especially if they're on another network that's gatewayed to the mailing list's network. The addresses in message headers can get completely rewritten or deleted.

Getting called an elitist snob

I take travel seriously. It's almost a religion for me. I've flown over the Arctic Circle; I've motorcycled around the Baltic Sea; I have friends in many parts of the world who share this passion for travel.

I contrast travel with tourism. To me, tourism is taking a bus tour, pointing at natives, and buying trinkets.

At one time, I subscribed to several travel mailing lists. In one travel group, I read the following exchange:

Person One asked what places to visit on an upcoming trip to Pennsylvania.

Person Two responded that Lancaster County was an interesting place and posted some in-depth comments about the Amish and their philosophy.

Person Three piped in, recommending the discount shopping malls in Lancaster.

I got upset at Person Three's comments and posted a long message about how travel should be taken seriously. I then lectured about how the Amish had wanted to get away from modern society and wasn't it ironic that they are now surrounded by crass materialism.

*In response, I got 5 or 6 strongly worded messages, basically telling me what an elitist ******* [snob] I was.*

(continued on next page)

It's a good idea to put your correct mail address in a signature at the end of your message. If the mailing list is available through the Internet, give your Internet address. Most email programs can automatically add a signature block to the ends of your messages.

Send a message to the subscribe address when you change your address or unsubscribe.

If you move to another computer, network provider, company, school... your email address might change. Some list management programs have a command for changing your address. If yours doesn't, unsubscribe at your old address and resubscribe at the new one.

To unsubscribe from a list run by a list management program, send a message to the list subscription address. The sidebar "Steps to subscribe or unsubscribe from a list" shows the procedure for unsubscribing.

If you have difficulty in unsubscribing, it is probably because the list server doesn't recognize you. The list server knows you by the complete email address from which you first subscribed.

This problem can be more subtle than it first appears. For example, my office has several computers. Most of the time I work on the one named "rock", but I can log on to "ruby" by clicking an icon, if I want to do some work on the other system. To the outside world, my email address is *lamb@ora.com*, no matter which machine I'm currently logged on to. However, if I subscribed to a list while logged on to rock, the list server would see my full address as *lamb@rock.west.ora.com*. If I were logged onto ruby when I tried to unsubscribe, the list server would see that unsubscribe command as coming from a "new" user, *lamb@ruby.ora.com* and send me an error message.

If you've saved your original email message that you sent to subscribe, you may be able to look back to see if your email address is different now than when you first subscribed. If your subscribing address is different from your current address, you can try to duplicate your original address (e.g., by logging in to another machine). If you can't duplicate the original address for unsubscribing, you can write to the list administrator, giving your old address and asking to be unsubscribed. (Refer to your original welcome message for specific instructions.)

Resources

For finding mailing lists

Mailing lists change frequently. New lists are added all the time; subscription or broadcast addresses can change. Since the information is changing all the time, use an online source to find lists you might be interested in.

- If you have a World Wide Web browser, use the following URL to see the 14-part (at last count) list currently maintained by Stephanie da Silva:

  ```
  http://www.cis.ohio-state.edu/hypertext/faq/usenet/mail/
  mailing-lists/top.html
  ```

- If your site gets Usenet newsgroups, you can use a newsreader program to look at the newsgroup *news.lists*, for the List of Publicly Accessible Mailing Lists.

Other Internet resources

- The "Internet Help Desk" maintains information on Internet tools such as mailing-list programs, as well as help documents on other topics. This resource is available for those with a World Wide Web browser, at the URL:

  ```
  http://gnn.com/gnn/helpdesk/basics/index.html
  ```

- You can request the "Newbie Guide to Internet Resources" by sending an email message. This guide includes information on using FTP, Listserv's, etc. Send mail to the following address with the subject: "send newbie":

  ```
  To: srea@uaex.arknet.edu
  Subject: send newbie
  ```

The story of "Jane Doe"

Pushing your own product on an Internet mailing list is not allowed. However, a list subscriber can mention a product she thinks would be useful to others in the group, usually with a disclaimer that she has no financial ties to the product or company.

On a mailing list for trainers, I saw a message praising a product from my company. The message gave my name as a contact for further information.

I was glad to see the message, because it might help our sales to other trainers on the lsit.

After reading the message, I sent mail back, very casually, to an address that I thought was the owner of the list. I said that it would probably be easier for the list owner to just post our company's discounts for trainers—if he wanted to do that—and proceeded to list the discounts.

Of course, the mail went to the whole list, instead. And it looked like I was using the mailing list to pump my own product.

Well, the list owner sent out a flame to everyone on the list, about how I—and our company—use underhanded tactics to sell our products, and how he for one would never buy from us.

I called him on the phone to explain and ask for some understanding for an honest mistake. The list owner ended up sending mail to the list, exonerating me and our products.

But it was quite an uncomfortable experience.

"Jane Doe"

CHAPTER 7

What you need to know to customize your environment

Every mailer has some settings that you can change.

Email programs are software programs created by people. The creators of email programs decide what features to include. For example, a common email feature is the ability to sort the list of messages.

The creators of email programs also decide what settings can be changed by a user and what defaults to assign—how a mailer will work "out of the box." For example, a user might be able to sort messages by date, sender, and subject; the default sort order might be by date received.

You can customize your mailer to select the settings that work best for you.

First, you need to learn what choices are open to you.

Mailers vary in complexity. A simple mailer might offer 20 basic functions. A more complex mailer could offer 70 or more.

Mailers vary in the amount of customizing they allow you to do for each function. One mailer might let you customize a few functions, while another might let you customize nearly every function in a wide variety of ways.

I save a copy of each mail message I send out.

Jerry Peek

Settings in graphical mailers

Macintosh Eudora

You are prompted with options every time you take certain actions, such as when you send a message (Cc, Bcc, send message right now) or when you start a search (match case, summaries only). These choices pertain only to the current action.

You can also change settings that apply to all messages. Click on icons on the Icon bar to select settings such as:

* Enable/disable a signature
* Word wrap
* Replacing tabs with eight spaces within the message body
* Quoted-printable encoding

Select Configuration from the Special menu to set:

* Window size
* Screen and print fonts
* The word-processing program to which you want to save messages

Select Switches from the Special menu to enable or disable:

* How you are advised of new mail
* What header fields you see
* Whether to leave mail on the server
* Other on-off options

cc:Mail

Most options are selected each time that you take an action, such as sending a message or starting a search. You are prompted for those options with check boxes or text fields in dialog boxes.

Select Options from the File menu to show settings that you can change for the entire session and subsequent times when you open mail, such as:

* Message display
* Confirmation of messages sent
* Fonts
* How you are notified of new mail and how often the mailer checks with the server for new mail
* How you display your message list
* Which SmartIcons to display and how to label them

The choices that you have under the File menu depend on the system your terminal is running on.

What you need to know to customize your environment

Mailers also vary in how easily you can discover what choices are available to you. It might be easy to discover your choices with a menu-based mailer where one of the menu items is Options or Configuration. It might be more difficult to understand how you can change things if you first need to discover what settings are called and what options are available before you can change anything.

Perhaps the best way to find out what your choices are (and which work best) is to ask a coworker who uses your mailer. For example, if you're going to be reading mail from Eudora from a home PC next week, ask someone who's already done this what you should change. If you like the way a coworker has set up Z-Mail to display message summaries, ask to see the definition in her setup file.

This chapter show you sample settings that you can modify. To know more about all the choices that are available in your mailer, refer to your online help system and/or the documentation that came with your mailer.

Configure your mail by making menu selections or editing a text setup file.

Most email programs are flexible and can be customized to work the way you want them to (more or less). The programs have a way for you to set and save the features you want.

In graphical mailers, you use menus and dialog boxes to control your mailer's settings.

In command-line mailers, settings are indicated and stored in a setup file that you edit with a text editor. Setup files are usually in your home directory. (You can also change settings temporarily on the command line of the mailer.)

Settings are either on-off or a user-supplied value.

A setting stores information that your email program needs. When you first start a mail program, each setting has a default that is presumed to be the one that most users will want. Each setting has a name, such as folder, askcc, or prompt.

Editing setup files for UNIX mailers

Where to find your setup file

If you use a UNIX mailer, setup files are usually in your account's home directory. The file or subdirectory begins with a period (or dot) and ends with "rc". Go to your home directory and list all the files, including the "dot" files that are usually hidden, with ls:

```
cd
ls -a
```

A common setup filename under UNIX is .mailrc; several programs read it. You might have both a .mailrc file and another "dot-rc" file such as .mushrc or .zmailrc.

What settings are available?

Different mailers let you control different settings. When you are in the Mush mailer, the command:

```
set
```

shows you all settings and their current values. The command

```
set ?all
```

shows you the list of settings and their definitions. For other mailers, check the help system for the correct commands.

On-off settings

If a setting is on, it appears like this:

```
set autosign
```

If a setting is off, it appears like this:

```
unset autosign
```

Other possible on-off settings are:

```
set verify
set ask
set hold
set askcc
set alwaysignore
```

Settings with user-defined values

You set values for some settings. For example, Mush and Z-Mail let you set the print command that you give within the mailer. In your .mushrc or .zmailrc file, you can set a value for the print command. The line:

```
set print_cmd = 'lpr -Pbrian-txt'
```

means that when you tell Mush (or Z-Mail) to print, the mailer will use the command lpr -Pbrian-txt.

Some other possible settings with user-defined values are:

```
ignore Received X-Mailer Status
set editor=vi
set folder=~/Mail
set ignoreeof='echo 'Use "quit" to quit.''
set editor=vi
set prompt=(%T) %f: #%m of %t>
```

Mail aliases

You can define aliases in this file, by listing the alias that you want to use followed by the full email address(es):

```
alias bradley bradley.ross@bamc.com
alias ron 0004300052@cmimail.com
alias buddies linda cathy donna
```

Command definitions

You can also define commands in a dot-rc file. For example, the command:

```
cmd del 's !* +deleted; d !*'
```

first saves a message to a folder called deleted, before deleting the message.

What you need to know to customize your environment

Like a light switch, a setting can be on or off. For example, Mush provides an on-off setting called askcc, which determines whether or not the mailer prompts you for the names of carbon copy recipients for your message. If askcc is on, Mush asks you if you want to send a carbon copy to anyone each time that you send a message. If the askcc setting is not on, Mush won't ask you about carbon copies.

Settings can also show values. For example, you might set the editor so that you can invoke it in email:

```
set editor = vi
```

Create a signature file that can be automatically placed at the end of messages you send.

When you send an email message, the mail system adds your From: address to the message header. If you want to add your phone number, an extra copy of your email address (for safety, in case some gateway ruins your address in the mail header), or a clever saying...you can do that with a signature file. The signature file is added to the end of each email message you send.

You indicate whether the signature setting is on or off. Before you can use the signature, you must supply the text. You decide what your signature says, whether it is

```
Ted Meister, ted@roa.com
```

or

```
Theodore Meister
graphic designer, O'Reilly & Associates
ted@roa.com
```

When you send a message, you won't see the signature print at the end of your message. Some mailers do notify you each time they append a signature file. Otherwise, the only way that you'll know that the mailer is including a signature is by the signature setting (or if you see a copy of your own message).

What modifications have you made to your mail program?

I have a Mac at home (as well as at work), which I use for my own design work. I often read email at home, particularly on the weekends. I have Eudora set up at home so that a copy of any new message is downloaded to my home Mac. The actual message stays on the server, so I can see it in my in-box at work the next day. Otherwise, Eudora would delete it from the server, and I would have no record of the message in my mailbox at work.

Anything I do with the messages I read at home is not reflected on the server or in my Eudora account at work. If I delete a message at home, it remains in my in-box at work. If I reply to a message from home, I have to remember to copy myself on it in the address line or I won't see my reply at work. Sometimes I forget, and then I have to go to my out-box on my home Mac and forward my reply to myself, so I can read it at work.

I have my Eudora Configuration file on my home Mac set to skip big messages. Otherwise, my modem will crash.

Edie Freedman

Creating a signature file

Mail programs let you set a signature in various ways. The signature can be one line or several. (Four lines is the recommended maximum.)

Macintosh Eudora

To create a signature, select Signature from the Special menu. Type your signature text in the window that is displayed. Save the entry.

Activate or deactivate a signature while you are using Eudora by clicking on the Signature icon on the Icon bar.

Set the signature to on or off by default by choosing Configuration from the Special menu and changing the signature setting.

MH

When you compose a mail message, MH reads a template file called components in your MH directory. Add your signature line(s) at the end of the components file, e.g.,

```
To:
cc:
Fcc:
Subject:
--------
-- Emma Thomas, ethomas@roa.com
```

Mush

For UNIX mailers, the standard place to put a signature file is a file named .signature in your home directory.

If you want to use a signature with Mush, enter your signature in a file that you name .signature in your home directory. (Note the "dot" or period at the front of the filename; you might have to use a list command option such as ls -a to see such "hidden" files.)

If you want to include a signature by default with each message, include this line in your .mushrc file:

```
set autosign
```

Mush and Z-Mail allow you to have two signature files. You could have one signature that you use within the company, and a more formal signature that goes to people outside the company.

To use a second signature, enter it in a file, such as .sig, in your home directory. Then add the line:

```
set autosign2=
```

to your *.mushrc* file. After the equal sign, list the machine names or addresses that you want to receive the second signature, then a colon and the filename of your second signature file. For example, to use a second signature file named .sig for all mail sent to addresses on the computer named roa, enter:

```
set autosign2=roa! @roa: ~/.sig
```

Check with your system administrator or help desk consultant if you have questions about system names at your company.

What you need to know to customize your environment

You can automatically save your outgoing mail.

Most mailers can be set to keep a folder with copies of all the mail you send. That means you won't need to remember to send a cc: to yourself. Of course, if you send a lot of mail, this folder can fill up pretty quickly; you'll need to remember to clean it out.

In Eudora, select Switches from the Special menu. Click on the Keep Copies check box so that a check mark appears. When Keep Copies is set, Eudora keeps a copy of all your outgoing mail in the Out mailbox.

In Mush, pick a folder name for your outgoing mail and set the record option in your .mushrc file:

```
# Save all messages I send in +outbox folder:
set record = "+outbox"
```

Remember that all folder names in Mush have to begin with a plus sign (+). (The line with the # sign in front is a comment line. You can place a comment line in the .mushrc file or other program file to help you remember what you were defining.) Automatic mail-saving will start working the next time you start Mush.

Specify your preferred word-processing program or text editor.

Some PC and Mac mail programs let you select a word processing program into which you save files. (When you save a mail message as a file, the file will be saved as a document in that word-processing application.) This setting can save you the extra step of having to open your favorite application and read in the text of the message.

For example, Macintosh Eudora lets you name such an application. First, select Configuration from the Special menu. There is a setting that reads "Application TEXT files belong to." Click the large button beneath this setting; select the word processing application you want from a file dialog box; then click on Open. The application of your choice will be entered in the Configuration dialog.

Creating commands to speed productivity

I manage a mailing list. I get in a large volume of mail, most of which is in the correct format and which I can forward to the program that handles the mailing list, listproc.

Since I forward so much mail, I have written an alias to shorten what I have to type. I use the custom command "mlp" to stand for:

m listproc@online.roa.com

Stephanie Davis

Some mailers let you specify the text editor that you use within the mail program while composing a letter.

For example, Mush lets you set an editor in the .mushrc file. The line

```
set editor = vi
```

means that as soon as you start a mail message, you will be in the vi editor. The line

```
set visual = vi
```

means that when you start a mail message, you will be in the mailer's simple editor. However, whenever you invoke a visual editor with ~v at the beginning of a line, you will go into the vi editor. (Only set one line or the other, depending on whether or not you want to always go automatically into the text editor.)

Set how often your mailer checks for messages.

Mailers that periodically check with a server for new mail addressed to you often let you set how frequently your terminal checks for new mail. For example, on Eudora, select Configuration from the Special menu and enter the time in the setting "Check for Mail Every __ Minutes."

Before you set this time to a more frequent interval than is entered by default, check with your documentation or with your local mail administrator. There might be a serious performance issue if you set the mail checks to occur too frequently. Often an interval of around 15 minutes is recommended as a minimum.

Set whether you want your mailer to alert you to new mail.

Many people don't want an alert when they get new mail. They find that such interruptions disrupt their train of thought, and they want to check for mail when it is convenient for them.

However, most mailers let you set an alert to tell you of new mail. You can set such an alert as a default, or only enable it when you are waiting for a critical message that you don't want to miss.

Alerts for most mailers are settings within the mailer itself. For example, in Eudora, select Switches from the Special menu. On that menu, you can select a number of on-off settings: Alert, Sound, Flash Menu Icon, or Open In Mailbox.

On UNIX systems, a program called biff can be set running in the background—outside the mailer—to monitor the size of your mailbox file. When the file changes size, the biff command sends you a message that you have new mail.

Set the order in which you see the list of messages.

The list of message summaries is in a default sort order, usually by date received. Some mailers let you make changes to this sort order.

For example, in cc:Mail, select the Options menu under File; then select Lists. You can choose to see last-received messages first or last messages last.

Mush offers you many more sort options. You can establish any sort option as the default by putting the appropriate line in your .mushrc file. For example, a line in the .mushrc file that reads:

```
set sort = sort -a -d
```

sorts messages by author and then by date received, and it displays your messages in that order when you open the mailer.

Set the display of header information in the list of message summaries.

In many mailers, you have no control over how the message summaries appear. In other mailers, there is a default display of information that you have some control over.

In Macintosh Eudora, the columns of information shown in the message summaries are status/priority, sender/recipient, date, size, and subject. You can change the width of any column by positioning the cursor on the divider, clicking, and dragging with the mouse. You can hide a column of information entirely, by shrinking the column as far as its left divider.

In some UNIX mailers, the display of message summaries is defined in the setup file in your home directory. In Z-Mail,

What modifications have you made to your mail program?

I have a simple signature file.

I also set up an alias called trav.info. I use the alias trav.info as the address that people reply to, whenever I widely post an announcement (in print, on mailing lists, etc.).

People who respond to the address trav.info get an automatic response that I've gotten their mail. Then I can go back through the messages that the announcement generates, more at leisure, and respond individually with further info.

That alias isolates my personal mailbox from a flood of inquiries that might come in.

Allen Noren

I changed the spacing and order of the columns of the message list. I wanted more space for the subject line.

Linda Walsh

Running biff on X

If you have an X terminal
or workstation, the name
of the command to use is
xbiff. If you want to turn
on xbiff by default, add
the line:

    xbiff&

to your .xsession or
.xinitrc file. (Add this list
above the last line of your
.xsession file; the last line
is reserved for a
command running the
xterm console window;
that command must be
listed last and must be run
in the foreground.)

Mush, Pine, and Elm, you can select what header information
you want to appear, in what order, and how much space it will
have. There is a default definition of the header information in
the setup file. (You probably won't be writing the setup file
from scratch.) For example, for Mush, a rather cryptic line such
as:

```
set hdr_format='%20a %M %-2N %5T (%3.51 li) %.20s'
```

defines the header summary format in the .mushrc file. This
sample definitions shows (after the message number and its priority) the sender's address (in 20 spaces), the month, day, time
(in five spaces), number of lines (xxxx), and the subject (in 20
spaces). For example:

```
20 A SREA@UAEX.ARKNET.E Dec 13 8:11 (1246 li) Re:send newbie
```

You can modify this line. For example, you might want to
delete the length of the message from the summary and add
ten spaces to the length of the subject:

```
set hdr_format='%20a %M %-2N %5T %.30s'
```

Or delete the length of the message and add five spaces to the
From: address and five spaces to the Subject:.

```
set hdr_format='%25a %M %-2N %5T %.25s'
```

Mailers sometimes show header fields that you might not want to see.

When you send a mail message, you don't see all the fields
that your header will contain when it is delivered. Your mail
program adds some fields when you send the message. Your
computer's mail system—and mailers along the way to the
recipient—also can change the header.

The best way to find out what your mail header looks like to
recipients is to send a message to yourself. If you have an
account on another computer, send mail to it to let you see
what happens as the message goes over a network.

Suppress extraneous header fields when you read or print out mail.

If you don't want to see fields like Received:, X-Mailer:, and
Return-Path: when you read a message, you can suppress

them. (In case you're wondering, those "useless" fields can be quite useful when you are troubleshooting network routing.)

In Eudora, select Switches from the Special menu and check that the setting Show All Headers is turned off.

For UNIX command-line mailers, add an ignore line to your .mailrc file. This line lists the header fields that you don't want to see when you display a message. For instance, to ignore fields which begin with Received, X-mailer, and Return-path, add this line:

```
ignore received x-mailer return-path
```

If you want to see these fields on your screen, but ignore them when you print a message with the Mush lpr command, use the -h switch:

```
Msg 4 of 13: lpr -h
printing message 4...(15 lines)
1 message printed at "laser".
```

This won't print the fields in your "ignore" list. The Mush command lpr -n ignores the entire header when you print a message; it just prints the message body.

Print with customized header and/or fonts.

Mailers have different "standard" ways that they print messages. Eudora automatically prints headers and footers for each message that you print, showing, e.g., the window, title, page number, and your address on each page. Eudora also lets you set a printer font and font size on the Configuration dialog box, under the Special menu.

UNIX command-line mailers often print in Courier or other constant-width font by default. The printed message doesn't scan too easily and sometimes it is difficult to separate your pages of print-out from other print-outs on the printer. You can customize printing in UNIX mailers, by adding a line to the setup file. For example, in your .mailrc file (or .mushrc, .zmailrc, etc.), you have, or can add, a printer setting:

```
set printer = 'lpr -Ppuck'
```

You can add options to this definition to customize your printing or to call another program to filter text through. If you aren't sure what printing options or programs (such as enscript

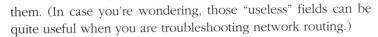

---

biff on Berkeley UNIX

If your system runs the Berkeley version of UNIX, you can turn biff on by typing at a system prompt (not within the mailer):

  % biff y

To turn off the biff program, type:

  % biff n

If you want the biff program on by default, add this line to your .login file:

  biff y

Information contained in a header

Here is a sample listing of a header that you might see at the beginning of a mail message. We have added a number before each field, to make talking about the fields easier.

1. From jpeek@roa.com Sun Apr 17 11:14:19 1994
2. Return-Path: <jpeek@roa.com>
3. Received: from roa.com by rock.west.roa.com (4.1/SMI-4.1) id AA07073; Sun, 17 Apr 94 11:14:16 PDT
4. Received: by roa.com (8.6.8/) id AB18272; Sun, 17 Apr 94 14:14:05 EDT
5. Message-Id: <199404171816.LAA04989@ruby>
6. From: jpeek@roa.com (Jerry Peek)
7. Date: Sun, 17 Apr 1994 11:16:46 PDT
8. To: lamb@rock.west.roa.com
9. Subject: Just testing
10. Cc: jpeek@roa.com

1-2. From (the first line, without a colon at the end) and Return-Path: are both added to your message to tell other computers who you really are (you can change the other From: field easily). It also tells other mailers where to send error messages (bounces and warnings).

3-4. Each computer that receives your message adds a Received: field with its complete address, the date and time, plus other tracking information. If there are delivery problems, this information helps in tracking them down.

5. Message-Id: is a unique number assigned to each message sent from your computer. As a message makes its way from computer to computer, the message-Id is stored in log files. If there are problems, this odd-looking field helps people identify your message in the flood of email that crosses most systems.

6. From: tells who the message is from and their email address. This line can have different formats, depending on your mailer and your system.

7. Date: tells the date, time, and time zone when the message was sent.

8. To: shows the email address, or the address of the mailing list or system-wide alias to whom the mail was addressed.

9. Subject: shows the subject header given to the message by the sender.

10. Cc: shows other recipients of the mail. (Cc stands for Carbon copy or Courtesy copy.)

Your system may show different fields in the header; ask your system administrator or post-master for help if you need it.

What you need to know to customize your environment

or mp) are available at your site, ask your system administrator or help desk consultant. Or, if you notice a coworker who is printing out good-looking mail messages, ask him what print command he has used.

You can read your mail remotely.

If you'll be away from your computer for a while, it can be nice to read your mail from wherever you are. If your office computer has dial-in modems and you have a personal or home computer with a modem, you can dial in to read your mail. (Or, if your computer has a direct Internet connection, you can use the telnet or rlogin commands from anywhere else on the Internet to read your mail.)

Some mailers make dialing in easier. For example, Eudora recognizes that sometimes you might dial in to see messages but might not want to permanently download your messages to the machine you dial in from. Select Switches from the Special menu and set Leave mail on server, if you want to keep your mail in one place. (You can also set "Skip Big Messages" if you have a slow modem.)

Another way to route your mail to another address is by setting up mail forwarding. When you do, messages that come into your computer are resent to you at another address. For example, if you are going to be at another office for a week, and want to be able to work locally on incoming mail instead of working over a remote login, you can forward your mail to a computer in that office that you have an account on.

With some mailers, you can define your own commands.

Maybe there's a series of steps you do all the time that you'd like to "automate" by putting them into a single command. UNIX mailers let you create your own simple commands to put in your .mailrc or other .rc file (.mushrc, .zmailrc, .mailxrc, etc.). For example, if you use Mush and want to define a new delete command, you can add a line to your .mushrc file to define the new command.

What modifications have you made to your mail program?

None. I tend not to do that. Even on the last system I used, where I was quite experienced, I still used standard stuff.

I was on a system where the mail software would frequently be amended. Then, whenever a new version came out, you had to redo the configuration.

Frank Willison

I have made a signature file and folders to store mail. I've modified the screen font, print font, and the columns of information that mail shows me.

Eudora gives you a lot of preferences to set.

I wish that I could control signatures more. I had been using a funkier signature, with a "cute" saying, but I kept forgetting to disable it when I sent mail to people who didn't know me.

After a few times of feeling embarrassed, I felt I had to make my one signature corporate and pretty boring.

Ted Meister

Changing the **UNIX** mailer prompt

With some UNIX mailers—Mush, Z-Mail, Elm, Pine—you can set the prompt to give you information such as the name of your current mail folder, the date and time, and more.

For example, the default Mush prompt we use at O'Reilly & Associates looks like:

(11:55) mbox: #1 of 6>

It has the current time (in parentheses), the folder name, the current message, and the total number of messages.

To change your Mush prompt, edit the line in your .mushrc file that defines the prompt; if there is no set prompt line, you can add one.

Any part of the prompt that stands for something changeable—like the name of your current folder—is written with symbols. These symbols look like %x —that is, a percent sign followed by a letter.

If you type:

help prompt

you will see the list of things you can put into your prompt. A partial list is:

Msg 1 of 6: help prompt

. . .

%f name of the current folder
%m current message number
%n number of new messages
%u number of unread messages
%d number of deleted messages
%t total number of messages

So, if you want to add the name of the current folder to your prompt definition, add the symbol %f.

If you want to experiment with setting your Mush prompt before you edit your .mushrc file, you can temporarily set the prompt while you are using Mush. Just type the set prompt command from a Mush prompt. It looks like this:

set prompt = "stuff you want in your prompt"

You will substitute the actual Mush prompt you want to use for the "stuff you want in your prompt." Put double-quote characters around the prompt. For example, you could set a Mush prompt to show the name of your current folder first, then the current message number, and the total number of messages.

set prompt = "%f msg %m of %t: "

The prompt would then appear:

mbox msg 2 of 3:

Once you get a prompt you like, you can use it every time you run Mush by putting a line defining your prompt into your .mushrc file:

set prompt = "%f msg %m of %t: "

In the same way, you can set a prompt in command-line Z-Mail (in the .zmailrc file), Pine (in the .pinerc file), or Elm (in the /.elm/.elmrc file).

Forwarding mail on a **UNIX** system

These procedures only apply if your computer uses the sendmail mail transport agent (and a few others that work like sendmail). If you aren't sure, ask your postmaster. Also, some sites restrict use of some or all of the things explained here.

If you're new with email, you should ask your postmaster before you try to set up mail forwarding. If you do it wrong, all your email can bounce or go into an endless loop.

To forward all your mail to another machine:

1. Find the complete address of the place you want your mail forwarded. This cannot be a personal alias (in your .mailrc file). Send a message to that address and be sure the message gets there okay; this will help you be sure that the forwarding will work.

2. Create a file in your home directory named .forward (the name starts with a dot). On the first line of the file, put the address you want your messages sent to. Don't put any boldfacing or other special characters in the file (make it a plain ASCII file).

    For example, to forward all your mail to linda@rock.west.roa.com, put this line in the .forward file:

    linda@rock.west.roa.com

3. Send an email message to yourself at your old (current) address. A minute later, rename the .forward file to temp.forward with the UNIX command mv:

    % mv .forward temp.forward

    That cancels forwarding temporarily.

4. Be sure that your message was forwarded to the new address. If it wasn't, find the problem and fix it.

5. If the forwarding worked, rename the file to .forward again:

    % mv temp.forward .forward

To cancel forwarding:

When you want to cancel forwarding, remove the .forward file. This is easy to forget (at least for me!). You might make a note on your calendar.

Here's another tricky way to remember: While you have the .forward file renamed to temp.forward (so mail isn't being forwarded), send yourself a mail message that reminds you to cancel the forwarding.

When you come back to your old address and start your mail program, the reminder message will be waiting there for you.

Make your own Mush commands

Here's a sample of how to create a new command with Mush.

Suppose that you don't want your "deleted" mail to be completely removed every time you quit Mush. You can define a new command called del. (The name is arbitrary; you can choose another name.) When you use del to "delete" a message, the message is actually saved to a folder named +deleted.

Every so often, you can clean out your +deleted folder (with the d command) to really delete the messages.

There's one catch: if you use the Mush s command to save a message out of any folder except the system mailbox, the message isn't removed from the current folder. So, after our del command saves a message to the +deleted folder, it will also use the d command to delete the message from the current folder.

Here's the line for your .mushrc file:

cmd del 's !* +deleted; d !*'

Let's take a closer look at that:

The cmd del means "this defines a command named del." The rest of the line is the definition: what you want the del command to do.

Put a pair of single quotes (' ') around the definition of the command.

The semicolon (;) separates the two individual commands we want del to do for us.

The first command, s !* +deleted, looks a lot like what you'd type if you wanted to save messages in the +deleted folder:

s 3-5 +deleted

But what's the !* business? That tells Mush to "replace the !* with any message numbers I type when I use this command." So, when you actually use your new del command at a Mush prompt:

del 2-4

Mush will replace the !* with the 2-4 you type. Then it will run s 2-4 +deleted.

If you don't type any message numbers when you use the command, like this:

del

then Mush will replace the !* with nothing—and it will run s +deleted, which will delete the current message.

So, again, when you define a cmd in your .mushrc file, put !* wherever Mush should plug in the message numbers.

The last part of the command, d !*, marks the messages for deletion after they've been saved into the +deleted folder. As with the s command, if the !* is replaced with the message numbers, if any. That's just one example of the commands you can define.

What you need to know to customize your environment

What you need to know to show off

Communication can be light-hearted, as well as useful.

Although you probably spend most of your computer time on business, there are times when you can relax and even be silly. This chapter shows some lighter ways in which you can communicate by email. As with all communications, remember to keep your audience in mind—what they understand, what they expect, how well they know you, whether they're paying to receive your email, and so on.

Smileys are sideways faces that you can use to indicate emotion.

The :-) is a smiley. Looked at sideways, it's a smiling face. It means "I'm just kidding." A smiley lets you add some of the facial expressions to your messages that people would see if they were with you in person.

Besides the most common smiley, there are plenty more, like:

;-)	Wink; sly grin
:-/	Resigned; so-so; disappointed but what can you do?
:-(	Sad; angry
8-O	Shocked; amazed

Why are smileys sideways?

Most people notice something sideways about the emotions expressed by smileys.

I meant to send flowers ;-)

I can say something, and then wink at you.

I'm slowing down. I don't look for adventure anymore. :-)

I can say something that's a bit cynical and then use a smiley to have a laugh and disavow it all at once.

Well, having no vacation simplifies my life quite a bit. :-(

A smiley tells someone what you really mean when you make an offhand remark.

Dale Dougherty
from the book Smileys
(O'Reilly & Associates)

Smileys are often placed after a sentence, so that they don't run into other punctuation.

I'm sorry I can't go to the movies with you. :-(

A different tradition for showing emotions evolved on CompuServe. Instead of smiley "drawings" people indicted their emotions more literally with <grin>, <gasp>, <roll on the floor laughing>, etc. in their text. Sometimes, <grin> will be shortened to <g>.

A word of warning: some people despise smileys. However, I've heard even avowed smiley-haters grudgingly admit that a smiley in a particular message was appropriate or clever.

As with anything else that you plan to put in your email, consider with whom you're communicating. For a general audience, you can use the basic smileys sparingly where they are helpful in communicating. For your friends who already know and love you, you can be more flamboyant.

Smileys can also be simple pictures.

Smileys can show not only emotions. There are smiley animals:

8)	Frog
3:-o	Cow
. \ /	Duck
=====:}	Snake
8:]	Gorilla

There are smileys of famous people and characters:

B-)	Batman
7:^]	Ronald Reagan
:-.)	Madonna
=):-)	Uncle Sam

There are hundreds of smileys, and most of them have more than one meaning. Don't count on people to understand the more obscure smileys.

Q:-)	New graduate
O-Z-<	In a big hurry
d:-)	Baseball player
:-x	Not telling any secrets

Email often contains acronymns.

Email and mailing lists are often acronym-rich environments, especially when technical subjects are being discussed. FYI, here are examples of a few acronyms that might show up:

BTW	By the way
FYI	For your information
FAQ	Frequently asked question
FOAF	Friend of a friend; used as a disclaimer when the writer can't verify the source
FWIW	For what it's worth
IMHO	In my humble opinion (also IMO)
MOTOS	Member of the opposite sex
MOTSS	Member of the same sex
RTFM	Read the f---ing manual
ROTFL	Roll on the floor laughing
TTFN	Ta-ta for now
TIA	Thanks in advance
TANSTAAFL	There ain't no such thing as a free lunch

Different email cultures (organizations, companies, or mailing lists) have their own vocabulary, which can include acronyms. Within that culture, some acronyms might be in frequent use and some acronyms might be met by a blank stare. As you read email, you'll pick up the vocabulary used by the group.

Signature files can turn into works of poetry or art.

Chapter 8 explains how to set up an automatic "signature" that's added to the end of your message. These signature files started out as a way to add your name, email address, and other information to the bottom of your message.

But you can do more with a signature file. You can add a saying—from Bartlett's, from a favorite movie or book, or from your own fertile imagination. You can add graphics created from typewriter characters. Or you can combine the two.

The next few pages show you how signatures can turn into an art form. Signatures can provide a place to make a statement, tell who you are, or show how clever you are.

Be courteous with your "clever" signature.

Your signature is generally part of each email message (unless you disable it or only invoke a signature on occasion). A signature contributes to the overall message you're trying to communicate. So here are rules to consider:

- Keep your signature brief. It's best to get across your point in as few lines as possible. Signatures over four lines long will be rejected by some news posting programs, so if you use Usenet, you'll need to have some kind of alternate signature. Even if you don't use Usenet, most sources say that signature files more than five lines long are considered impolite and to be avoided.

  All art forms have their constraints; the constraint for a signature that you use every day is its length.

- Keep your signature appropriate. While you're thinking up a great, funny signature that your friends will love, remember who else will be seeing the signature. In many mailers, once you create your signature file, you won't see the signature unless you copy yourself on mail.

  Zmail and Mush mailers let you create two signature files and specify who will receive which signature; that way you can have a formal signature for the world and an informal signature for closer friends/colleagues.

- Remember that you have a signature and review it occasionally. Have you changed titles or phone numbers? Is it time to revise that tired quote that everyone must have seen dozens of times? Some people keep a file of alternate signatures and refresh their signature files frequently.

- Make it uniquely yours. The whole point of personalizing a signature file is to say something about yourself. It is considered bad form to copy someone else's signature exactly, only changing the name.

Check your signature file for portability to different computers.

When you create your signature file, remember:

- If you put special formatting in your signature, don't make it wider than 65-70 characters. On some peoples' systems, the lines will be broken (wrapped) and your signature will turn into junk.

- Don't use tabs in your pictures. Tab characters won't look the same on other peoples' screens as they do on yours. Note that some editors, like vi, automatically convert multiple spaces to tabs in some cases.

- Don't leave extra spaces at the ends of lines. For example, this clever signature came from an ORA person, before she read this book. ;-)

```
 \\      |\.-./|
  \\     |'a a'|     Cynthia Pribram
   \\ =(= v =)=    O'Reilly & Associates, Inc.
    \\ / _^_/\     103 Morris St * Sebastopol, CA

     \\| \_/  |
      \ || || /
      (_|| ||_)
        ^^  ^^
```

The line with the street address had so much white space at the end that the spaces "wrapped" around to the next line; the cat seemed to be broken into two pieces on my screen. Her screen was wide, so the cat didn't look "broken" to her. It did to other people who read her messages, though.

- The font (style of characters) on your screen may not look the same as it does on other peoples' screens. If you want people to really appreciate your work of art :-) , be sure it looks right on several different brands of terminals.

When you create your signature, use a constant-width (type-writer-style) font. In these fonts, all characters, including spaces, have the same width. That makes it easy to create columns of characters and to make things line up.

Drawing email pictures

I use Eudora on a Mac.

When I first saw smileys, I started making some funny little face drawings by picking odd characters from the Mac's character set. Other Mac users who read my mail saw what I had intended and thought the pictures were neat.

However, when I sent mail to users on X terminals, I had problems. It seems that one of the characters I picked in my funny little picture triggered an attachment when read in Z-Mail. People who used Z-Mail couldn't read the first line in my message unless they displayed a file attachment.

The lesson is: if you are drawing email pictures, only use the ASCII characters or the picture may screw up when sent to a another machine.

Larry Watson

Signatures

Signature files can show the world your address and contact information, but they can also show some personality.

```
    peter.schmitt@dartmouth.edu                    {   }
    UNIX Systems Specialist                        {   }
    603-646-2085          _____        \|/      ++   /
          _____  |_____|__/-\__|-|_^_/-\__||_n ====
    n_____/           \_ |[][] |-----------------|----| \
    | Live Free or Die  || 221 |_____|_|| |    Computing Services
    |     +UNIX+         | ------/ ==__---_  ====--||-      Dartmouth College
    q|===================|_|=====__/ =======|=====[__]-p    Kiewit Comp. Ctr.
    _____( )( )_____( )( )_____\ /_\ /_\ /          Hanover, NH  03755
```

New Hampshire is a state in the US with a State motto of "Live free or die!" This signature equates technical freedom with political freedom.

```
    ~~~~~~~~~~~~~~~~~~~~~~~~~~~~~~~~~~~~~~~~~~~~~~~~~~~~~
    Tony Thomas                                  /
    thomas@math.purdue.edu                     0)%___    /
    '92 BMW K75S                            __/ (BMW) ===#_
    Eat and sleep as much and as well as possible.  / /\\|||L/~~\\
                                              \__/ --- \__/=~~
    ~~~~~~~~~~~~~~~~~~~~~~~~~~~~~~~~~~~~~~~~~~~~~~~~~~~~~
```

Tony's signature is sometimes seen on the BMW mailing list for motorcycle fans.

```
                                       .            ,
                                              .:/
    Rosemary Dean Mackintosh         .     ,,///;,    ,;/
    rosemary@clam.rutgers.edu        .    o:::::::::;;///
    "Set the gearshift for the high gear of your soul!"   >::::::::::;;\\\
                                          ''\\\\\'" ';\
                                            ';\
```

Rosemary's signature was taken from a band. "I am a big fan of the band Phish, hence the fish, and the quote from Phish's song 'Antelope'."

```
    _____      !  _____
    Chris Casey                        | |
    chris_casey@kennedy.senate.gov    /''''\
    http://www.ai.mit.edu/people/casey/casey.html  /_____\
                                      |@@@@@@@@|
    202/224-3570                      ||0||0||0|
    Office of Senator Kennedy    _____/_____ " " " " _____/\_____
    Washington, DC  20510       {|| || || || || ___/\____|| || || || ||}
    _____{|_||_||_||_||__/__/\__\__||_||_||_||_||_|}
```

Signatures can emphasize your employment.

```
    _/\ _ !\ _           @         Milwaukee, WI - A Great Place On a Great Lake
    ! _! !! ! !_  ~~  @ ~ ~~
    ! ! ! !! ! ! !~~__=||_~ ~~~ Computing Services Division - MAINFRAME CONSULTING
    ! ! ! _! ! ~~~ ~\____/  ~~~  yanoff@csd4.csd.uwm.edu yanoff@cs.uwm.edu
```

Signatures can describe where you are.

```
    jnelson@iastate.edu
    Four
    Lines
    Suffice.
```

Signatures can be very simple but still clever.

```
    Scott Senften                    senften@shell.com
    Shell Development Company, Bellaire Research Center
    3737 Bellaire Blvd., Houston, TX 77025
    (Voice: 713 245-7167)

       /////
      | @ @   "All the other nations are drinking Ray Charles beer,
    c _)     and we are drinking Barry Manilow." - Dave Barry
      \ o
```

Signatures can be constantly changing and evolving.

"I collect sigs, and try to rotate mine periodically. I try to keep where I got them. Also, you probably know this but, there is some great stuff on rec.arts.ascii."

A sampling from Scott's collection of quotes:

```
    -------------------------------------------------------
    "The most exciting phrase to hear in science, the one that
    heralds new discoveries, is not 'Eureka (I found it)' but
    'That's funny...' "
    --Isaac Asimov
    -------------------------------------------------------
    why is sky blue [r=135, g=206, b=235]
    -------------------------------------------------------
    "There ain't no rules around here!
    We're trying to accomplish something!"
    --Thomas Edison
    -------------------------------------------------------
    "Put not your trust in Kings and Princes.
    Three of a kind will take them both."
    --General Robert C. Schenck
    -------------------------------------------------------
    The absence of alternatives clears the mind marvelously
    --Henry Kissinger
    -------------------------------------------------------
    One does not grow older at the table
    --Old Italian Proverb
    -------------------------------------------------------
```

If you aren't sure whether you are using a constant-width font, type these three lines onto your screen:

```
          |
iiiiiiiiii|
WWWWWWWWWW|
```

The first line has ten spaces and a vertical bar. The second has ten i's and a vertical bar. The third line has ten W's and a vertical bar. If the three vertical bars line up, you have a constant-width font.

- Don't make characters that flash, are boldfaced or highlighted, etc. Use plain text. That's because not everyone has the same kind of terminal you do; the special hidden commands that look one way on your terminal may look like garbage on someone else's screen.

When you send mail, it "hops" from computer to computer.

Your computer does not need a direct connection to another computer to send electronic mail to that computer. Nor does your computer need to be on the same network as the computer you are sending mail to. Your computer can be connected to the Internet and someone else's computer can be connected to CompuServe. Since the Internet and CompuServe "talk to" each other, you can send mail to that person.

When you send mail, your computer passes the message to another computer. Mail is passed from computer to computer until it reaches its destination. The "hops," or relays, that mail passes through vary by where the mail is going, the load on the systems, and so on.

The sidebar "Tracing the route of a message" shows an example of the hops that a mail message might go through before it is delivered.

You can check when mail is delivered.

You can count on email being delivered. If there are problems with delivery, you'll get an error message. Even so, it can be interesting to look "behind the scenes" to make sure mail is actually delivered to the target computer.

The mailer Eudora has a "Show Progress" option as part of its Configuration menu. This option shows you messages about where the mail is going (although these usually go by so fast that you're not quite sure what you saw). For very large files, such as messages that include complicated graphics, you can see the time that it takes for them to be sent and check that they are delivered.

Most UNIX mailers allow you to use a "verbose" option when you send mail. The verbose option lets you see the messages that your computer exchanges with the target computer and see that the mail has been delivered successfully. For example, within Mush, you can send mail with the command:

```
mail -v kate@nws.baug.bg
```

Normally, you would just get your mail prompt back again. However, with the -v option, you see more information first:

```
Signing letter... /home/lamb/.signature: 1 line
Sending letter ... kate@nws.baug.bg... Connecting to
rs.baug.bg. (smtp)...
220 rs.baug.bg Sendmail AIX 3.2/UCB 5.64/4.03 ready at Fri,
11 Nov 1994 22:59:59 +0200
>>> HELO rock.west.roa.com
250 rs.baug.bg Hello rock.west.roa.com
>>> MAIL From:<lamb@roa.com>
250 <lamb@roa.com>... Sender is valid.
>>> RCPT To:<kate@nws.baug.bg>
250 <kate@nws.baug.bg>... Recipient is valid.
>>> DATA
354 Enter mail. End with the . character on a line by itself.
>>> .
250 Ok
kate@nws.baug.bg... Sent (Ok)
Closing connection to rs.baug.bg.
>>> QUIT
221 rs.baug.bg: closing the connection.
sent.
```

cc:Mail has a Receipt option that you can check when sending a mail message. If you check the Receipt option, you will get a message back when the recipient reads the message.

Resources

This chapter can't cover everything that you might want to know about smileys or creating graphics. There are online and print resources available if you want to know more:

How do you express yourself in email?

I communicate mostly with retail bookstore buyers.

My signature file has a box, my name and numbers, and a quote. Everyone in the stores loves the quotes. My current one is "If I were a dog, I wouldn't succumb to humanity."

I always refer to dogs in my quotes. I make up a new quote and put it in my .signature file every two months.

Hugh Brown

Smileys

A complete list of smileys can be found online. If you have a Gopher client, you can give the command:

```
gopher spinaltap.micro.umn.edu
```

Your computer will retrieve a file from a computer at the University of Minnesota. On the screen, you will see a menu of choices. Select Fun from the first menu, Humor from the second menu, and Smileys from the third.

If you don't have a Gopher client, you can rely on the printed word. The small book *Smileys* (O'Reilly & Associates) contains 650 smileys in its reference section. There are listings by subject matter, examples of usage, games like a smiley "word search," a program to generate random smileys for signature files, etc.

Acronyms

If you have access to a WWW browser, you can look up a collection of acronyms and meanings at:

```
http://www.ucc.ie/info/net/acronyms/acro.html
```

If you don't have access to a WWW browser, you can ask questions about an acronym by sending an email message. To find out about this email service, send a mail message to *freetest@iruccvax.ucc.ie*. Leave the Subject: field blank and put the word "help" in the first line of your message:

```
To: freetext@iruccvax.ucc.ie
Subject:

help
```

Creating graphics

Graphics created from typewriter characters are also referred to as ASCII art. (ASCII code is a set of 128 characters recognized by a computer system.)

If you can read Usenet at your sight, start by looking at the newsgroups *alt.ascii-art* or *rec.arts.ascii*.

Tracing the route of a message

On a UNIX system, system administrators sometimes use the traceroute command to see the hops that a message would take from one computer to another. For example, the following shows the route from a computer terminal in Sebastopol, CA to the computer at American University in Bulgaria:

1   ora-west-gw.west.roa.com (198.112.209.2) 3 ms 3 ms 3 ms
2   198.112.210.5 (198.112.210.5) 86 ms 92 ms 88 ms
3   nearnet-gw.roa.com (198.112.208.2) 89 ms 88 ms 90 ms
4   bbn1-gw.near.net (131.192.52.1) 460 ms 242 ms 248 ms
5   mit2-gw.near.net (131.192.2.2) 120 ms 112 ms 117 ms
6   192.54.222.8 (192.54.222.8) 125 ms 111 ms 110 ms
7   Boston3.MA.ALTER.NET (137.39.100.97) 116 ms 125 ms 112 ms
8   Boone1.VA.ALTER.NET (137.39.128.6) 126 ms 142 ms 125 ms
9   icm-dc-1-E4/1.icp.net (192.157.65.225) 134 ms 181 ms 262 ms
10 icm-dc-2b-F1/0.icp.net (144.228.20.103) 153 ms 218 ms 206 ms
11 icm-paris-1-S0-1984k.icp.net (192.157.65.130) 849 ms 923 ms 696 ms
12 Paris-EBS1.Ebone.NET (192.121.156.9) 966 ms 798 ms 744 ms
13 Vienna-EBS1.Ebone.NET (192.121.156.18) 681 ms 731 ms 1137 ms
14 cisco.baug.bg (192.121.159.58) 2464 ms 3187 ms 2494 ms

Mail from O'Reilly's office in Sebastopol (line 1) is first routed to our company's computer in Cambridge, MA (line 2). Our network provider is Nearnet (lines 3, 4, and 5), which sends the message on to Alternet. The Virginia Alternet computer (line 8) then sends the message across the Atlantic, where it goes through Paris and Vienna (lines 12 and 13) before ending up in Bulgaria.

Even a message that is sent to a person nearby can end up following a complicated route. For example, sending mail from one computer terminal to another in the San Francisco Bay area can still entail a cross-country journey, depending on how the computers route the mail. This example traces a route from a computer terminal in Sebastopol to a terminal about an hour's drive away:

1   ora-west-gw.west.roa.com (198.112.209.2) 18 ms 3 ms 3 ms
2   198.112.210.5 (198.112.210.5) 98 ms 87 ms 87 ms
3   nearnet-gw.roa.com (198.112.208.2) 89 ms 91 ms 88 ms
4   bbn1-gw.near.net (131.192.52.1) 536 ms 299 ms 345 ms
5   mit2-gw.near.net (131.192.2.2) 302 ms 225 ms 259 ms
6   192.233.33.6 (192.233.33.6) 324 ms 159 ms 118 ms
7   t3-3.cnss48.Hartford.t3.ans.net (140.222.48.4) 115 ms 292 ms 113 ms
8   t3-2.cnss40.Cleveland.t3.ans.net (140.222.40.3) 178 ms 282 ms 160 ms
9   t3-2.cnss25.Chicago.t3.ans.net (140.222.25.3) 137 ms 317 ms 148 ms
10 mf-0.cnss11.San-Francisco.t3.ans.net (140.222.8.195) 504 ms 378 ms 194 ms
11 cnss12.San-Francisco.t3.ans.net (192.103.60.6) 200 ms 187 ms 465 ms
12 enss314.t3.ans.net (192.103.60.70) 263 ms 247 ms 334 ms
13 199.182.126.2 (199.182.126.2) 220 ms 492 ms 216 ms
14 netcom.netcom.com (192.100.81.100) 410 ms 337 ms 427

CHAPTER 9

What you need to know to send files

You can successfully email plain text files to anyone.

Previous chapters have talked about sending and receiving messges with text only. Email systems were originally designed to handle only ASCII text—English language letters, punctuation, and other symbols. Plain ASCII text is still the lowest-common denominator for email. If you send a message to a valid email address, with only text, the recipient will be able to read it correctly.

However, people want to send all kinds of files to all kinds of people in all kinds of places. They want to send graphics files or audio files or video clips or program source files. And they want to be able to send files to someone else regardless of what kind of computer or email program that recipient has.

This chapter looks at some of the issues that you have to think about when you're sending non-ASCII files by email.

The ideal world: you can instantly share any file with any recipient.

Almost any file can be sent by email: a program, a data file, a picture or sound, etc. Features for email programs, such as

The real world

It would be nice if sending files by mail was seamless and transparent. Unfortunately, it often is not.

What you end up needing to do is experiment with file formats and what works.

Ron Petrusha

The historical limitations of ASCII text

Left to themselves, computers only speak binary numbers—0 or 1 (on or off). So to represent characters, like A or Z, you need an encoding system that represents each character as a unique binary number.

Early in the development of computers, there were several competing codes, but the one that has become the widespread standard for representing the English alphabet is called ASCII, which is short for American Standard Code for Information Interchange.

It turns out that you only need seven bits of data to give you all the codes you need to represent the English language—the letters, punctuation marks, and numbers used in English text. Using seven binary digits gives you 2^7, or 128, unique codes.

```
0000000 0000001
0000010 0000011
0000100 0000101
0000110 0000111
0001000 0001001
0001010 0001011
0001100 0001101
0001110 0001111
```

and so on. Each of these codes is assigned to an English letter, punctuation mark, or other character. For example:

```
a = 1100001    $ = 100100
b = 1100010    ( = 101000
A = 1000001    , = 101100
B = 1000010    . = 101110
```

Because most early communications programs were concerned only with sending ASCII text, it became commonplace to assume only seven bits were available. (The eighth bit of a standard byte was used for a now-obsolete form of error-checking called parity.) As a result, early email designers realized that they could rely on seven bits as the least common denominator.

The problem is that this seven-bit standard makes it difficult to send non-text data—computer programs, images, the "extended ASCII," used to represent the additional characters used in some European languages, and so on—by email.

The way around this problem is to make the non-text data look like ASCII. There are a number of mathematical techniques for mapping eight-bit codes onto ASCII's seven bits—and these techniques have been applied in various "handmaidens" to electronic mail—programs like uuencode, or btoa. The resulting file is readable ASCII, but looks like garbage! For example, this is what a uuencoded file might look like:

```
M1G)0;2!L86UB($UO;B!&96(@,C @,#DZ,30Z-#<@,3DY-0
M"E0.B!E;&QE;@I3=6)J96T.B!%;%;;6%I;"!C;W!Y9611=',*1&%%T93
M+" R,"!&96(@,3DY-2 P.3HQ-#HT-R!04U0*"DAI($5L;&5N+ H
M:6YG(&%R92!M>2!C;VUM96YT<R!O;B!Y;W5R(&0<'EE9&ET<R!
M<'1E<G,,@@"TX+&@270G<R!0.V%Y('=I=&@@;;64@@%:68@@=V
M92!0<FE;%@@I09B!C:8%P=&55R<R W(&%%%N9" X+& $@5&AE('-
M>&%%M<&QE<R!A="!!T:&4@96YD"D]F(&4@;871871P97(@(@R!A<F4
M<;;VYG(&'I!L86-E++ @;5&&AE>2!S:&H]U;&0@;0;8F$4*"(G(&(@
```

attaching documents, are becoming more common because there are standard ways of doing them.

Some electronic mail systems allow you to mail files as separate entities along with a message. That is, when you send a message to somene you can say: "send this file, too." When the message is read, the receiving mailer asks the person reading the message where the file should be stored. These files can be either binary or ASCII, and system information about the file is preserved in the move. For example, you could send a message saying "Take a look at the spreadsheet I've enclosed and get back to me," and attach an Excel spreadsheet from a Macintosh. When the recipient reads the message and accepts the attachment, his Mac automatically creates an Excel spreadsheet file on his machine.

The real world: the recipient may find a file unusable when it arrives.

To transfer a non-ASCII file, you first pack it safely for travel through networks—typically compressing and encoding it into ASCII—then send it via your mailer. Some mailers can perform the compression and encoding for you automatically.

For the recipient to be able to use a file received through email, the file must pass a number of hurdles:

- The file has to be small enough in size for the recipient's mailer to deal with.

- The file has to have been uncorrupted in its travels.

- The recipient needs the right software to be able to decode the file. (The decoding might be done automatically by the recipient's mailer, or the recipient might have to go through manual steps of decoding and then uncompressing.)

- The recipient has to have the application that the file can be read with.

The basic rule: check with your recipient first.

If you're sending a file to someone for the first time, check what kinds of files they can receive. You'll save yourself and your recipient time and headaches if you think of sending a file

as a two-step process: first decide how you're going to communicate and then send the file.

People get into trouble when they assume that somone else's system is just like theirs. For example, if you can receive a large graphic file with no problem, don't assume that everyone else can receive such large files. If you have a PostScript printer, don't assume that everyone can print PostScript. Or, if you use binhex to encode files, don't assume that everyone does. (Like travel, sending files across networks is broadening.)

You'll want to ask your recipient:

- Can you receive this size file?

- Do you have the program needed to read or view this file?

- Of the ways that I can encode and send you this file, which can you receive? (Depending on the similarities between the sender's and the receiver's environment, this will be more or less easy.)

First ask what the recipient's limit on message size is.

Every user has a certain amount of disk space on which to receive incoming mail. The space limit can be set by the system administrator, by physical space on a disk, or by the email program.

If you send a file that is too big for the mailer to read, the recipient's mailer probably will give him an error message, and he won't be able to read what you sent. In some cases, the mailer can freeze and prevent him from reading not only your message, but any other mail.

What size file is too big? That varies widely; a limit might be 32K or 1Mb or 100Mb. The only way to know the size limit is to ask.

- Some people have small, strict space limits for their mail account.

- Some people pay for "connect time" to receive messages and work over a slow modem, so a very large file might be a financial imposition or cause their modem to crash.

Some people won't know their size limit in kilobytes or megabytes. However, you can probably get an idea by asking about the kinds of files they have received without problems in the past.

If a file is too big to be handled by your recipient, consider compressing it with a compression program, breaking the file into smaller pieces, putting the file on a server to be retrieved by FTP or other software, etc. If necessary, you might even need to resort to sending a file on a disk through the postal mail.

Does your recipient have a program that will run, read, or view your file?

This question is easy to understand. If you're sending an Excel file, does your recipient have a copy of Excel with which to read the file? If you're sending a GIF file, does your recipient have a GIF viewer? Does it matter if you have two different releases of the same software?

The only time you might forget this question is when you assume that someone else's environment is like yours. If you don't have compatible software, you'll have to find a common denominator in which to exchange information.

Knowing your recipient's size limit and programs, how will you send the file?

There is still the problem of getting a message unscathed through network gateways. The only information guaranteed to arrive intact over a network to another person's mailer is ASCII text. So you need to have a way of encoding your non-ASCII file into ASCII, so that it can travel safely and your information can arrive as you intend.

In some instances where you and the receiver share the same local environment, you won't have to worry about sending a file. For example, if you are on a PC, using cc:Mail and sending a file over your local network to another user with cc:Mail on a PC, you can just use cc:Mail's file attachment selection and send the file.

However, if you're sending a file across networks, you do have to worry about your message getting unscathed through network gateways. The only information guaranteed to arrive intact over a network to another's mailer is ASCII text. So you

Resend mail

need to have a way of encoding your non-ASCII file into ASCII, so that it can travel safely and your information can arrive as you intend.

There are standard ways of encoding files to ASCII (and decoding them again on the other end):

- MIME is one standard that is available in at least some mailers on any operating system—PC, Macintosh, or UNIX—and that works across operating systems.

- If you and the recipient can't both use MIME, you'll have to find compatible compression and encoding programs that both you and your recipient can use. There are a variety of "standards" that apply to only one operating system or the other, and a few standards that work across operating systems.

Sending files with MIME is relatively easy (as is sending files within your local network), once you get a little experience with your mailer. Finding compatible programs can be more difficult to figure out, but you can find a way to transfer files, even so.

We expect more mailers to support MIME standards in the future. This will make file transfers easier.

If sender and receiver both have MIME-compliant mailers, transfer the file as part of a MIME message.

MIME (for Multi-purpose Internet Mail Extensions) patches most of the holes in the "text-only" email system. MIME was designed to get messages safely through network gateways that change a message to fit their own standard formats.

If you and your recipient both have mailers that can handle it, MIME is usually the best way to send files to each other. You can send files to each other safely, no matter what kind of computers you each use or what networks the files will travel through. And, you won't have to worry about compressing the files or encoding them to ASCII. The MIME-compliant mailers take care of all that for you.

Email programs that support MIME include Z-Mail, Eudora, and Pine. So, if you run Z-Mail on a PC and want to send a file to someone who uses Eudora on a Mac or who uses Pine on a UNIX machine (for example), you can do this.

If your email program doesn't support MIME, you might ask your system administrator about a freely-available package called Metamail to let you use MIME.

With MIME, you can send a variety of files as attachments.

What kinds of messages can MIME send?

- Plain text

- Formatted text (with boldfacing, italics, different fonts and point sizes)

- A partial message (MIME can split long messages into parts, then collect all the parts as the recipient gets them and put them back into a single message)

- Non-text (pictures, sound, data)

- Instructions to automatically get other files by anonymous FTP or from a mail server. (Instead of sending a huge file through email, the person who sends a message can ask MIME to send instructions for getting the file directly. The recipient's MIME mail reader will ask the recipient whether she wants to fetch the file; if she does, MIME will handle the details.)

- Alternative message parts. (For example, a MIME message can contain a message in two styles: as a fancy formatted PostScript file, and as plain text. If your mailer can't show a PostScript file, it will show the plain text automatically.)

- A combination of the above

MIME can pack all that stuff into plain-text mail messages that can make it unscathed through all mail gateways and can be read with email programs on many different operating systems.

MIME works its magic by using special header line to tell the receiving mailer how to handle the attached message—which might include launching a separate program to decompress a file or launching a GIF viewer to display an image.

Check with your recipient

My brother-in-law has a friend who works at a software company. One night, as a "favor," this friend sent him a game—a 200MB software package—by email.

The huge email message froze up his hard disk. He had to have his administrator remove the file on the server downstairs.

Linda Mui

Finding common denominators across systems

If you're sending a file, you'll first want to know if your recipient can receive a file of that size and can run the application.

SENDER

I want to send a 1 Mb jpeg file. Will your mailer accept a file of that size? Can you display a jpeg file?

I want to send a two page Postscript file. Can you print it?

I want to send you a six page Word file. Can you read it?

RECEIVER

Yes, I get jpeg files all the time. My mailer can receive it and I can view it.

Yes, I have a LaserPrinter that prints Postscript.

No. Can you save it as ASCII text and mail me that instead?

Once you know that you and the receiver have a common file application, if you both have MIME-compliant mailers, you can send the file that way.

SENDER

My mailer is MIME-compliant. Is yours?

RECEIVER

Yes.

The MIME-compliant mailer takes care of encoding the file before sending it; the receiver's MIME-compliant mailer decodes the file.

encodes files for safe travel over mail networks

decodes files

It doesn't matter if the sender or receiver has a Eudora mailer on a Macintosh or PC, Zmail on any platform, Pine on UNIX, etc. As long as the mailers can send and receive MIME messages, you can send files back and forth.

running on a Macintosh

running on a UNIX system

If you don't both have MIME-compliant mailers, you need to perform your own compression and encoding to pack files for safe transmission across network gateways. Your recipient has to unpack the files at the other end.

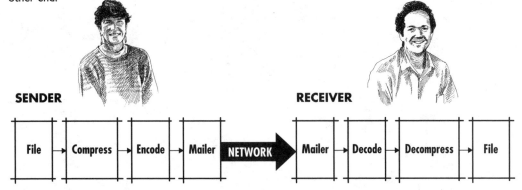

SENDER   **RECEIVER**

| File | → | Compress | → | Encode | → | Mailer | NETWORK➤ | Mailer | → | Decode | → | Decompress | → | File |

You need to have the same compression and encoding programs, as well as the same file application.

SENDER (Macintosh)   **RECEIVER** (Macintosh)

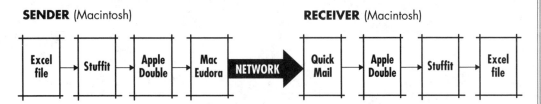

| Excel file | → | Stuffit | → | Apple Double | → | Mac Eudora | NETWORK➤ | Quick Mail | → | Apple Double | → | Stuffit | → | Excel file |

The sender is a Macintosh user with an Excel file. She uses Stuffit to compress the file, AppleDouble to encode it, and then sends the file through her mailer. The receiver gets the file in her mailer, saves the message as a file, decodes the file with AppleDouble, and uncompresses it with Stuffit. The receiver can then open the file in Excel.

SENDER (PC)   **RECEIVER** (UNIX)

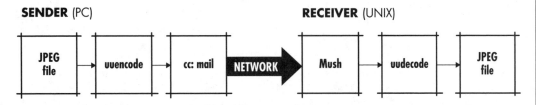

| JPEG file | → | uuencode | → | cc: mail | NETWORK➤ | Mush | → | uudecode | → | JPEG file |

Or, the sender is a PC user who needs to send a jpeg file over the Internet to a receiver on a UNIX machine. After discussing what decoding programs they have in common, the sender encodes the file with UUCODE and mails it. (A jpeg file is already compressed.) The receiver decodes the file with uudecode (a UNIX version of the program the sender used) and then displays the jpeg file with a viewer.

With a MIME-compliant mailer, you attach a file while composing a message.

If you have a MIME-compliant mailer, you can send any file attachment to another user, so long as that user:

- Has a MIME-compliant mailer
- Can receive a file of that size
- Has an application to use the kind of file you are sending, e.g., Word, GIF, Lotus 123, etc.

While you are composing a message, indicate that you want to attach a file. Then indicate the filename and make any encoding choices.

For example, while composing a message with Macintosh Eudora, select Attach File. A file dialog box appears; indicate the name of the file and then specify an encoding method. Depending on your version of the software, the choices could be:

```
MIME
Binhex
Uuencode
```

If you don't know of a reason for another preference, keep the default setting as MIME. There might be a reason to select another encoding method. For example, if you send a file with uuencode, the recipient need not have a MIME-compliant mailer to decode the message, only a uudecode program, which is standard on UNIX systems.

With graphical Z-Mail, while composing the message, select Attachments. Select a file, a file type, and an encoding method. After you click on the Send button, Z-Mail collects all the files into one message and does any encoding needed.

How to recognize a MIME message if you receive one.

Even if you don't use MIME yourself, you may still receive a MIME message.

In general, a MIME message has MIME-Version: and Content-Type: lines in its header. For example:

```
To: jpeek@ora.com
Subject: Meeting Agenda
MIME-Version: 1.0
Content-Type: text/plain
```

If you see header fields like those, you won't necessarily need a MIME-capable mail program to read the message. Because the message bodies are plain text, it's safe to look at them with your mail program. In a lot of cases, you'll be able to read them as they are.

MIME messages can have multiple parts.

The Content-Type field in header tells you what kind of content is in the message body.

```
To: jpeek@ora.com
Subject: Meeting Agenda
MIME-Version: 1.0
Content-Type: MULTIPART/MIXED; BOUNDARY="Boundary (ID
jrUgor2xiu492thM01CK0Q)"
```

MULTIPART/MIXED means that the message has more than one part ("MULTIPART") and that there's more than one type of content ("MIXED"). A multipart message has a boundary between the parts. The boundary starts with two dashes (--) and a boundary string. The MIME mail reader has to be able to tell where the boundaries are in a multipart mail message.

Each part starts with its own Content-Type: header. This tells your mail reader how to display (or process) the contents of that part. Line 10 tells that the first part of the message is plain text and it uses the US-ASCII character set. (MIME can handle international character sets, too.)

Since a MIME message is broken into parts, your mailer can read the plain text sections, even if it cannot read an attachment.

If you're sending a file to someone in a dissimilar environment, you'll have to be more creative.

If you can use MIME in a mail program, at the sender's end, your mailer automatically encodes the file into ASCII. At the recipient's end, his mailer automatically decodes the file and then uncompresses it.

Audio attachment

If you can't use MIME, you'll need to manually compress the file and encode it into ASCII; your recipient will have to manually decode the file.

You'll have to check with your recipient to make sure that he has any programs that will be needed to uncompress and decode the file. For example:

```
I have a 1MB GIF file, compressed with WINZIP. Can you deal
with that kind of file? Let me know if you would need
another graphics file format, or if you need me to use
another compression program.
```

If you both use the same operating system (e.g., Windows, Macintosh or UNIX) you should be able to find compression or encoding programs in common.

If you are on different operating systems—e.g., you are on a Macintosh and your recipient is on a PC with Windows—you will need to look harder to find common programs. (If you both had a MIME-compliant mailer, such as Eudora, MIME encoding would be your first choice.) If MIME is not an option, look for other cross-system standards, such as gzip and UUCODE (uuencode).

Once you have figured out the best way to exchange files with someone, you won't have to check the next time, unless something has changed.

Compression programs save space by reducing redundancy.

ASCII files often contain a lot of redundancy—repeated characters, long strips of white space, and so on. Other types of files, such as graphic bitmaps, may have even more repeated characters. It is possible to save a lot of space by using special encodings that let you eliminate the redundancy. This is the function of programs like compress, PKZip, gzip, and so on. They can reduce the size of some files by more than two-thirds.

This reduction in size is a good thing if you want to send a large file over a low-speed modem link. However, compressed files are binary files, so they need to be re-encoded as ASCII using a program like uuencode.

When you do compress a file, however, your recipient will have to uncompress the file at the other end. That means that whatever compression program you use, your recipient will also need to have access to it.

If you are sending a file from your PC to another PC user, a common compression file format is Zip; Windows users often have WINZIP or ZIPMANAGER; DOS users often have PKZip. If you are sending a file from Mac to Mac, Stuffit or Compact-Pro are common compression programs. If you are sending a file from a UNIX terminal to another UNIX user, compress is a common program.

If you are sending a file *between* operating systems—UNIX to PC, PC to Mac, etc—then you have to find a program that is the lowest common denominator between the two operating systems. gzip is one such program that is available for all three operating systems. However, gzip is not installed as a standard utility on all systems. If you don't have it at your site, ask your system administrator to install it; gzip is freely available over the Internet.

Before you send a binary file, encode it.

Encoding a file means that you have to convert all non-ASCII characters to ASCII, so that they can travel safely by email over networks, without being changed *en route*. For example, if you want to safely send a Macintosh file, and preserve its resource forks and data forks, you'll need to use an encoding program.

Whenever you encode a file with a program, remember that your recipient has to have access to the same program in order to decode the file that you send.

Some encoding programs (or file attachments) work only in certain environments. For example, if you send a file from one Mac to another Mac, you can encode the file with Binhex. If you send a file from a UNIX terminal to another UNIX user, you can use btoa.

However, if you're sending a binary file across operating systems, you will need to use an encoding program that can be used on both systems.

MIME is a system of encoding standards that works across operating systems, between users with MIME-compliant mailers.

If all else fails

A colleague keeps trying to send me a large Word for Windows file (2.5 to 3Mb). He has tried to send it to my MCI mail address and to my Internet address.

Somewhere in transit, the file becomes uuencoded. It is always bungled. I can't uudecode it.

When I've looked at the file, 1 byte is randomly dropped from the message and replaced by a linefeed character.

We don't know what the problem is. He's still trying. I suppose if this goes on long enough, he'll send a disk through the postal mail.

Ron Petrusha

Quoted-printable text

Some mailers, such as Eudora, give you an option of selecting Quoted-printable text. If you're wondering what this is...

Quoted-printable text is a standard that allows you to send non-ASCII text, such as Hebrew or Kanji characters.

US ASCII text is also called 7-bit text because each character takes seven bits of computer data. Seven bits allows enough combinations to uniquely identify every character of most alphabets. However, some character sets—like Japanese Kanji and Hebrew—require more than seven bits of data. Japanese Kanji, for example, has over 20,000 unique characters. MIME and other standards can squeeze these other character sets into a 7-bit format, so you can send them in a mail message.

Here's a message with Spanish characters in it:

> From: Linda Lamb <lamb@roa.com>
> To: carlos@entelfam.cl
> Subject: Estoy en Lima
> MIME-Version: 1.0
> Content-Type: text/plain; charset=ISO-8859-1
> Content-Transfer-Encoding: quoted-printable

The Content-Type: field has charset=ISO-8859-1. This tells MIME that the message body has characters in the ISO 8859-1 standard format.

The line Content-Transfer-Encoding: quoted-printable means that the Spanish characters will be represented in a special format of equals signs (=), letters and numbers.

If your MIME mail reader can display Spanish text, those characters would be shown in Spanish instead of the encoded characters.

For example, a message encoded as:

> Carlos, estoy en la casa de mi amigo. Pero, =Alqu=E9 d=EDa
> dif=EDcil! Tom=E9 un taxi entre al aeropuerto y el hotel.

would appear like this:

> Carlos, estoy en la casa de mi amigo. Pero, ¡qué día difícil! Tomé
> un taxi entre al aeropuerto y el hotel.

Sending a PostScript file by email

A PostScript file is an ASCII file—all its characters are keyboard characters—so technically, you can send it by email. However, if you've ever looked at the size of PostScript files, you know they can be very large, even for a file that prints out as only one or two pages.

If you want to send a PostScript file in an attachment, you need to know whether the recipient has a PostScript printer or a PostScript viewer (such as ghostview) and whether she can comfortably handle the size of file that you'll be sending.

If you want to include a PostScript file as part of a mail message, you'll want to help the recipient save and print or view the file correctly. To print correctly, PostScript files must begin with a PostScript header on the very first line:

```
%!PS-Adobe-2.0 EPSF-1.2
%%Creator: O'Reilly 2.1
%%CreationDate: 12/12/94 14/12/40
%%Bounding Box:126 142 486 651
%%End Comments
/ld {load def} bind def
/s /stroke ld /f /fill ld /m /moveto ld /l /lineto ld /c /curveto
ld /rgb {255 div 3 1 roll 255 div 3 1 roll 255 div 3 1 roll setrgb-
color} def 126 142 translate
360.0000 508.8000 scale
/picstr 19 string def
152 212 1[152 0 0 -212 0 212]{currentfile picstr readhexstring
pop} image
FFFFFFFFFFFFFFFFFFFFFFFFFFFFFFFFFFFFFFFF
FFFFFFFFFFFFFFFFFFFFFFFFFFFFFFFFFFFFFFFF
FFFFFFFFFFFFFFFFFFFFFFFFFFFFFFFFFFFFFFFF
FFFF8000EE614FFFFFFFFFFFFFFFFFFFFFFFFFFFF
FFFF00000000000000000000000000000FFFFFFFF
FFFF0000000000000000000000000000000FFFF
FFFF00000000000000000000000000000800FFFF
FFFF80000000435C7FFFFFFFF600001FFFFFFFFF
```

Even a blank line at the beginning of a PostScript file can prevent it from printing.

Before a recipient can print a PostScript file, he needs to delete any lines in the file above the required first PostScript line and delete any trailer lines after the PostScript file such as a signature. You can help this process by disabling your signature before sending a PostScript file, and by starting the message with an explanation of what the recipient needs to delete. Many people use a "cut here" marking to indicate what the recipient should delete.

> Here's the PostScript file we talked about. Save this to a file, and delete all beginning lines, up to and including the "cut here" mark before printing. Call me if you have any problems.
> -------------- cut here --------------
> %!PS-Adobe-2.0 EPSF-1.2
> %%Creator: O'Reilly 2.1

Online services that started out as standalone services are moving onto the Internet. They are now offering email across the Internet.

[At the time of publication...] there still can be substantial limits for users of those online services. For example, a user with AOL email can attach a file or document, but only to send to others on AOL. If a user tries to send an AOL attachment over the Internet, the recipient won't get that attachment.

On the receiving end, AOL has two limitations: it is not MIME compliant and it still has a 32K limit on messages.

If you were to send a MIME file to an AOL user, the AOL mailer would split the file into segments of 32K and would show any MIME code (for a graphic, etc.) as a block of text that looks like gibberish.

Online services will be increasing their message limits and becoming MIME compliant in response to user needs. The question for email users is: how soon?

John Labovitz

If both sender and receiver cannot use MIME, versions of the uuencode program (called UUCODE on DOS or WINCODE on Windows) are available for PC, Mac, and UNIX operating systems. These programs can work across operating systems, as long as you each have a copy of uuencode for your operating system.

If you can't use MIME across operating systems, use a standard like uuencode.

Even without MIME, it is possible for any mailer to transmit a binary file, provided that both the sending and receiving computers have a utility to convert binary files into some ASCII representation.

One universal utility for converting files to ASCII is uuencode. All UNIX systems have this utility. It is available for Windows, DOS, and Macintosh.

Uuencode does translate nonprintable characters into plain ASCII text. However, since mail gateways can still occasionally munge uuencoded files, use MIME if the recipient can handle it.

To include uuencoded file in your message, first create the uuencoded file. Then go into your mail program, start the mail message, and read in the file. Unless you need to save the uuencoded file, remember to delete it after you send the message.

If you get a file in a mail message and the person doesn't tell you that it's uuencoded, see whether it ends with this line:

```
end
```

and starts with a line like this:

```
begin 644 filename
```

If it does, it's probably a uuencoded file.

To extract a uuencoded file, first save the message in a file. (Be sure to use a different filename than the name on the "begin" line at the top of the file. When you extract the file, it is given the filename on the "begin" line. If there's a file with the same name in the current directory, it'll be overwritten. One easy way to keep filenames straight is to save the uuencoded file with a suffix or extension that identifies it. For example, if you get a uuencoded message with the first line "begin 600 ch01," its filename is ch01; you could save the file as ch01.uu to identify the file as uuencoded.

Give the uudecode command that works on your system.

On a UNIX system, use a left angle bracket (<) and the filename of the saved mail message. For example, to extract the ch01 file from a mail message saved as ch01.uu above:

```
% ls
ch01.uu
% uudecode < ch01.uu
% ls
ch01 ch01.uu
```

Resources

There is an online resource of information about MIME. The MIME FAQ (Frequently Asked Question list) can be accessed in several ways. The list deals with basic information, such as decoding MIME messages, using uuencode with MIME, conventions, security issues, etc., as well as sources for freely available and commercial MIME packages, and advanced topics. To obtain the MIME FAQ:

- If you have Mosaic, use the URL:

  ```
  http://www.cis.ohio-state.edu/hypertext/faq/usenet/mail/
  mime-faq/faq.html
  ```

- If you can read Usenet news, read the *comp.mail.mime* newsgroup. The FAQ is also posted to *news.answers*.

Sending binary files

I work on UNIX. If I want to send a binary file—a GIF file, compressed file, or sound file—to another person on UNIX, I run uuencode; the other person will have to run uudecode.

If I want to send several files, I do a tarfile, compress, and then uuencode.

If the file isn't too big, I just include it with my message, and do a "cut here."

But if you do that, you have to worry about the size, and the headers and footers.

Linda Mui

A UNIX-to-UNIX standard: btoa

The uuencode and uudecode programs aren't as reliable as they could be. Some UNIX systems have a newer program, btoa (pronounced "b to a"). btoa means "binary to ASCII"; it's used, like uuencode, to encode non-text files before you mail them.

btoa is a program only for UNIX users sending a file to other UNIX users; it is not available on all UNIX systems. Before you use btoa, be sure that the recipient also has it.

Here's a mail message with a btoa-encoded file:

```
To: mlee@ora.com
From: Jerry Peek <jpeek@rock.west.ora.com>
Subject: A Da Vinci painting
Mitch, here's a copy of the file I was talking about, Mona Lisa.
Feed it through "btoa -a":
xbtoa Begin
F(KG9@;-
j*G<lo.FE9T)+EqZc3S<*W@<Wi9ATDj'+Du+8FWbla0JGXG+Eo
Oq0JGXE0Hb70GB4+4ATT
&9ARfgFH?2hP;b1RVBJL QE+*cq4aM!lAkYT
;aa&G:f't^:f1&&1C@u-ES.dr3%u+q6>1BKS>j3j+
Eeks+D;+!@;m>@+E&2X2/+W]S>j3j+=eQD0FDZ*ES-
W@+@T]_)a 6_)[^FjES-WO+@T]d)a 6d)[^F
jES-V[+@T]g)a 6g)[^FjES-WQ+?FQs/h/
MZ<@0@<S>j3j+=_1M3ccr,.PG%#-8-;FD..B+.W6GJ%3
&(MD..B+.ShO_%3&(MD..B,+;c4?3cejTDJrrt+EqZcOH4F-
D..B,+:]M53cejT@;-j.D*9it@Ouu7
xbtoa End N 310 136 E 71 S 55d1 R 416bec53
```

Encoding btoa files

To include a message with the encoded file, first create the btoa -encoded file. Use the shell's right angle bracket (>) operator and pick a temporary filename:

```
% btoa < monalisa.gif > mitch.btoa
```

Now go into your mail program and start the mail message. Then use the command to read in the encoded file—for example, ~r mitch.btoa.

Unless you need to save the encoded file, remember to delete it after you send it.

Decoding btoa files

If you get a file in a mail message and the person doesn't tell you that it's processed with btoa, see whether it starts with this line:

```
xbtoa Begin
```

and ends with a line such as:

```
xbtoa End N 310 136 E 71 S 55d1 R 416bec53
```

If it does, it's probably a btoa-encoded file.

To extract this kind of file from a message:

- Save the message in a file:

```
s monalisa.btoa
```

- Quit your mail program and get to the UNIX shell prompt.

- Pick a filename for the file to be extracted. The btoa -a option extracts a file from a btoa-encoded message. Use a left angle bracket (<) and the filename of the saved mail message. Then use a right angle bracket (>) and the name of the file you want to create.

For example, to extract the ch01 file from the mail message we saved as ch01.btoa above:

```
% ls
monalisa.btoa
% btoa -a < monalisa.btoa > monalisa
% ls
monalisa
monalisa.btoa
```

What you need to know to send files

A UNIX-to-UNIX compression standard: tarmail

If you are a user on a UNIX system and are sending mail to a user on another UNIX system, you can compress files with tarmail, before sending them with the btoa or uuencode program.

Many UNIX systems have a program called tarmail; it uses the UNIX tar and compress programs. If you don't have tarmail, your system administrator can install it.

tarmail advantages

- tarmail works well with multiple files, packaging up one or multiple files into a compressed tar archive.

- The tar program lets you combine files (or links, symbolic links, and more) from one or more directories into a single archive. The file permissions, owners, and last modification time are preserved. When the archive is extracted, the contents will be recreated the way they are on your system.

- If the file is big, e.g., more than 700 lines, tarmail splits the file into pieces and mails each piece separately.

- The compress program squeezes down the size of the tar archive.

- The program makes mailing a lot easier.

Some versions of termail don't send any instructions to the recipient. If you use tarmail, be sure that the recipient knows what to do. (You can send a separate message with instructions before you run tarmail.)

Sending files with tarmail

The tarmail program needs three things on its command line, in this order:

- The address you're mailing the archive to.

- The subject of the mail message. Put double-quote characters (" ") around the subject.

- The names of the files you want to send.

For example, to send the files named ch01 and ch02 to lee@roa.com, give the command:

```
tarmail lee@roa.com "Chapters 1 & 2" ch01 ch02
```

To send the file(s) to more than one person, add the other addresses with commas, but no space, between the addresses.

Receiving files with tarmail

Extracting files from tarmail messages isn't as easy as sending them. The steps are:

- Be sure you have all the mail messages with the parts of the archive by checking the subjects. For example, if you get messages "Year-end figures part 1 of 3" and "Year-end figures part 3 of 3", you know that you're missing one of the parts.

- Save the parts—in numerical order—to a temporary file, without the message headers. For example, with most UNIX mailers, use the w command (which doesn't save the message header to the file) instead of the s command.

- Quit the mail program.

- Plug the temporary filename (here, jerry.tmp) into the command line below. If you have a System V (AT&T) UNIX system, use tar xovf instead:

```
% atob jerry.tmp | uncompress | tar xvf -
x ch01, 54829 bytes, 108 tape blocks
x ch02, 19383 bytes, 38 tape blocks
```

- Ignore the message about "tape blocks." If you get other messages you don't recognize, ask an expert for help.

Hint: If you want to see what files will be extracted before you extract them, change tar xvf to tar tvf.

Index

set visual command, 96
settings, mailers (see customizing email
    programs)
setup files, 91–92
sh command, 45
shell escapes, 45
Show Progress option (Eudora), 113
signature files, 93, 94, 107–112
    computer portabilty, 109, 111
    guidelines for, 108
signatures, automatic, 84
SmartIcons, 4
smileys, 105–106
    online source for, 114
sorting messages, 36
    by date, 57
    by priority, 48
sound files, 117, 127
Sprintmail, 67
storing incoming messages, 50
Stuffit compression program, 129
style tips for writing messages, 29–30
subject headers, 7
    changing, 55
    keeping same during email
        discussion, 25
    searching for words in, 37
    when replying to messages, 26
    (see also message headers)
Subject: header field, 100
SUBSCRIBE request, 78
subscribing to mailing lists, 77, 81
    Listserv, 84
    phrasing requests, 80
    problems with, 75
subscription addresses, 78–81
summary (see message summary)
suppressing header fields, 98
system errors and bouncing mail, 68
system prompt, 2
system-wide aliases, 45–48
    warning about, 46

tab characters, 109, 111
    problems using in messages, 29
tarmail, 135
threads, discussion, 25

To: header field, 24, 69, 100
top-level domains, 62–63
traceroute command, 115
tracing message routes, 115
troubleshooting
    bounced and undeliverable mail, 69
    checking addresses with verify, 70

uncompressing files (see compressing
    files)
undeleting messages, 8–9, 11
undeliverable messages, 65
UNIX
    btoa program, 134
    checking addresses with verify, 70
    command-line mailers in, 5
    compress program, 129
    location of incoming messages in, 50
    lpr command, 8
    pathnames, 54
    prompts, 102
    setup files, 91–92
    shell escapes, 45
    system prompt, 2
    tarmail compression standard, 135
    text editors, 44
    verbose option, 113
UNSUBSCRIBE request, 78
unsubscribing to mailing lists, 80–81
    when your address changes, 86
    (see also subscribing to mailing lists)
uppercase letters, 29
Usenet resources, 87
UUCP, 67
uudecode, 126, 129, 133–134
uuencode, 126, 128, 132–134
    versus btoa, 134

-v switch, 113
VAXmail, 15
verbose option (UNIX), 113
verify command, 47, 70
vi editor, 44, 96

warning messages, 65
white space, 30
windows, multiple, 45

About the Authors

Linda Lamb has been an email user since 1984, when she started with the program *mail* for interoffice communication. She still prefers command-line mailers, because they are fast, flexible, and don't require mouse clicks.

In past incarnations, Linda has been an administrator for group insurance, an organic farmer, a legal editor, a technical writer, a marketing communications manager, and always a mother. Having worked for the past ten years at O'Reilly & Associates, she is now an editor with a focus on user books.

Outside work, Linda is interested in science fiction/fact and other reading, choir, crafts, spiritual growth, and beginning a cooperative housing community.

Jerry Peek has used UNIX and email since the early 1980s. He has a B.S. in electronic engineering technology from California Polytechnic State University. In the years since, Jerry has worked as a user consultant for UNIX and VMS, developed and taught UNIX courses, administered a VAX 11/780 running BSD UNIX, and hacked Bourne Shell and C language code. He's now the Online Services Manager for O'Reilly & Associates, Inc.

In his copious :-) free time he hikes and bicycles the California coast and travels to obscure places in Latin America.

Colophon

Our look is the result of reader comments, our own experimentation, and feedback from distribution channels. Distinctive covers complement our distinctive approach to technical topics, breathing personality and life into potentially dry subjects.

In the What You Need to Know series, we look at technology in a personal way: how real people get something done and how they think about issues. The covers of the series reflect this personal, immediate approach to the subject. Inside the books, illustrations of the speakers in the sidebars give faces to those who have shared their experiences.

Edie Freedman designed the cover of this book, using an illustration by David White, in the style of 19th-century engravings. The cover layout was produced with Quark XPress 3.3 using the ITC Garamond and Futura fonts.

The inside layout was designed by Jennifer Niederst and implemented in FrameMaker 3.0 by Mike Sierra. The text and heading fonts are in the ITC Garamond and Garamond Condensed families. The sidebar text and headings are set in the Gill Sans font. The portraits were illustrated by Leslie Evans.

INTERNET

Books from O'Reilly & Associates, Inc.

SUMMER 1995

The Whole Internet User's Guide & Catalog

By Ed Krol
2nd Edition April 1994
574 pages, ISBN 1-56592-063-5

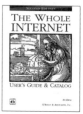

The best book about the Internet just got better! This is the second edition of our comprehensive—and bestselling—introduction to the Internet, the international network that includes virtually every major computer site in the world. In addition to email, file transfer, remote login, and network news, this book pays special attention to some new tools for helping you find information. Useful to beginners and veterans alike, this book will help you explore what's possible on the Net. Also includes a pull-out quick-reference card.

"An ongoing classic."
—*Rochester Business Journal*

"The book against which all subsequent Internet guides are measured, Krol's work has emerged as an indispensable reference to beginners and seasoned travelers alike as they venture out on the data highway."
—*Microtimes*

"*The Whole Internet User's Guide & Catalog* will probably become the Internet user's bible because it provides comprehensive, easy instructions for those who want to get the most from this valuable electronic tool."
—David J. Buerger, Editor, *Communications Week*

"Krol's work is comprehensive and lucid, an overview which presents network basics in clear and understandable language. I consider it essential."
—Paul Gilster, *Triad Business News*

WebSite™

By O'Reilly & Associates, Inc.
Documentation by Susan Peck & Linda Mui
1st Edition May 1995
ISBN 1-56592-143-7, UPC 9 781565 921436
Includes two diskettes, 342-page book, and WebSite T-shirt

WebSite™ is an elegant, easy solution for Windows NT 3.5 users who want to start publishing on the Internet. WebSite is a 32-bit World Wide Web server that combines the power and flexibility of a UNIX server with the ease of use of a Windows application. Its intuitive graphical interface is a natural for Windows NT users. WebSite provides a tree-like display of all the documents and links on your server, with a simple solution for finding and fixing broken links. You can run a desktop application like Excel or Visual Basic from within a Web document on WebSite. Its access authentication lets you control which users have access to different parts of your Web server. In addition to Windows NT 3.5, WebSite runs on the current version of Windows 95. WebSite is a product of O'Reilly & Associates, Inc. It is created in cooperation with Bob Denny and Enterprise Integration Technologies, Inc. (EIT).

WebSite is for anyone who wants to publish information on the Web, including individuals, corporate desktop users, and small and medium-size businesses and groups. The intuitive nature of the software and the comprehensive, easy instructions in the book make WebSite a natural choice for a wide variety of users.

The Website package includes a 32-bit HTTP server, WebView™, Enhanced Mosaic 2.0, and complete documentation.

Internet In A Box,™ Version 2.0

Published by SPRY, Inc. (Product good only in U.S. and Canada)
2nd Edition June 1995
UPC 799364 012001
Two diskettes & a 528-page version of
The Whole Internet Users Guide& Catalog *as documentation*

 Internet In A Box™ is the first shrink-wrapped package to provide a total solution for PC users to get on the Internet. Quite simply, it solves Internet access problems for individuals and small businesses without dedicated lines and/or UNIX machines. Internet In A Box provides instant connectivity, a multimedia Windows interface, and a full suite of applications. New features in the second edition include: access to the CompuServe Network; Spry Mosaic, Mail, and News; Secure HTTP; and a Network File Manager.

New features of version 2.0 include:

* More connectivity options with the CompuServe Network.
* With Spry Mosaic, browsing the Internet has never been easier with Progressive Image Rendering.
* SPRY Mail provides MIME support and a built-in spell checker. Mail and News are now available within the Mosaic Toolbar.
* You'll enjoy safe and secure shopping online with Secure HTTP.
* SPRY News offers offline support for viewing and sending individual articles.
* A Network File Manager means there's an improved interface for dealing with various Internet hosts.

For details about purchasing the upgrade, contact O'Reilly by pointing your Web browser to : *http //www.ora.com* or call us at 707-829-0515 or 800-998-9938.

Connecting to the Internet

By Susan Estrada
1st Edition August 1993
188 pages, ISBN 1-56592-061-9

 This book provides practical advice on how to get an Internet connection. It describes how to assess your needs to determine the kind of Internet service that is best for you and how to find a local access provider and evaluate the services they offer.

Knowing how to purchase the right kind of Internet access can help you save money and avoid a lot of frustration. This book is the fastest way for you to learn how to get on the Internet. Then you can begin exploring one of the world's most valuable resources.

The Mosaic Handbooks

Mosaic—the hot, new, point-and-click graphical interface—is becoming instrumental in the growth of the Internet. These books—one for Microsoft Windows, one for the X Window System, and one for the Macintosh—introduce you to Mosaic and its use in navigating and finding information on the World Wide Web. They show you how to use Mosaic to replace some of the traditional Internet functions like FTP, Gopher, Archie, Veronica, and WAIS. For more advanced users, the books describe how to add external viewers to Mosaic (allowing it to display many additional file types) and how to customize the Mosaic interface, such as screen elements, colors, and fonts. The Microsoft and Macintosh versions come with a copy of Mosaic on diskettes; the X Window version comes with a CD-ROM.

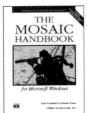

The Mosaic Handbook for Microsoft Windows

By Dale Dougherty & Richard Koman
1st Edition October 1994
230 pages, ISBN 1-56592-094-5
(includes Enhanced NCSA Mosaic on two diskettes)

The Mosaic Handbook for the X Window System

By Dale Dougherty, Richard Koman & Paula Ferguson
1st Edition October 1994
288 pages, ISBN 1-56592-095-3
(includes Enhanced NCSA Mosaic on CD-ROM)

The Mosaic Handbook for the Macintosh

By Dale Dougherty & Richard Koman
1st Edition October 1994
198 pages, ISBN 1-56592-096-1
(includes Enhanced NCSA Mosaic on diskette)

Managing Internet Information Services

By Cricket Liu, Jerry Peek, Russ Jones, Bryan Buus & Adrian Nye
1st Edition December 1994
668 pages, ISBN 1-56592-062-7

This comprehensive guide describes how to set up information services and make them available over the Internet.
It discusses why a company would want to offer Internet services, provides complete coverage of all popular services, and tells how to select which ones to provide. Most of the book describes how to set up Gopher, World Wide Web, FTP, and WAIS servers and email services.

"*Managing Internet Information Services* has long been needed in the Internet community, as well as in many organizations with IP-based networks. Although many on the Internet are quite savvy when it comes to administering these types of tools, *MIIS* will allow a much larger community to join in and perhaps provide more diverse information. This book will be a welcome addition to my Internet shelf."
—Robert H'obbes' Zakon, MITRE Corporation

TCP/IP Network Administration

By Craig Hunt
1st Edition August 1992
502 pages, ISBN 0-937175-82-X

TCP/IP Network Administration is a complete guide to setting up and running a TCP/IP network for administrators of networks of systems or lone home systems that access the Internet. It starts with the fundamentals: what the protocols do and how they work, how to request a network address and a name (the forms needed are included in an appendix), and how to set up your network.

Beyond basic setup, the book discusses how to configure important network applications, including sendmail, the r* commands, and some simple setups for NIS and NFS. There are also chapters on troubleshooting and security. In addition, this book covers several important packages that are available from the Net (such as *gated*). Covers BSD and System V TCP/IP implementations.

"*TCP/IP Network Administration* provides a great service to network managers. Any network manager responsible for TCP/IP networking should keep a copy of this inexpensive reference nearby."
—*Network Computing*

Using Email Effectively

By Linda Lamb & Jerry Peek
1st Edition April 1995
160 pages, ISBN 1-56592-103-8

When you're new to email, you're usually shown what keystrokes to use to read and send a message. After using email for a few years, you learn from your own mistakes and from reading other people's mail. You learn:

- How to organize saved mail so that you can find it again

- When to include a previous message, and how much to include, so that your reader can quickly make sense of what's being discussed

- When a network address "looks right," so that more of your messages get through the first time

- When a "bounced" message will never be delivered and when the bounce merely indicates temporary network difficulties

- How to successfully subscribe and unsubscribe to a mailing list

With first-person anecdotes, examples, and general observations, *Using Email Effectively* shortens the learning-from-experience curve for all mailers, so you can quickly be productive and send email that looks intelligent to others.

Marketing on the Internet

By Linda Lamb, Tim O'Reilly, Dale Dougherty & Brian Erwin
1st Edition Fall 1995 (est.)
170 pages (est.), ISBN 1-56592-105-4

Marketing on the Internet tells you what you need to know to successfully use this new communication and sales channel to put product and sales information online, build relationships with customers, send targeted announcements, and answer product support questions. In short, how to use the Internet as part of your overall marketing mix. Written from a marketing—not technical—perspective, this guide gives marketing and sales people a model for thinking about what you can do online, in terms of activities you are already familiar with.

Every company has some valuable information to give away that will provide a motive for people to visit your online site. You'll succeed with this new channel if you start using the Internet as part of your overall marketing mix and build on your experience over time.

MH & xmh: Email for Users & Programmers

By Jerry Peek
3rd Edition April 1995
782 pages, ISBN 1-56592-093-7

There are lots of mail programs in use these days, but MH is one of the most durable and flexible. Best of all, it's available on almost all UNIX systems. It has spawned a number of interfaces that many users prefer. This book covers three popular interfaces: *xmh* (for the X environment), *exmh* (written with tcl/tk), and *mh-e* (for GNU Emacs users).

The book contains:

- A quick tour through MH, *xmh*, *exmh*, and *mh-e* for new users

- Configuration and customization information

- Lots of tips and techniques for programmers—and plenty of practical examples for everyone

- Information beyond the manual pages, explaining how to make MH do things you never thought an email program could do

- Quick reference pages in the back of the book

In addition, the third edition describes the Multipurpose Internet Mail Extensions (MIME) and describes how to use it with these mail programs. MIME is an extension that allows users to send graphics, sound, and other multimedia formats through mail between otherwise incompatible systems.

sendmail

By Bryan Costales, with Eric Allman & Neil Rickert
1st Edition November 1993
830 pages, ISBN 1-56592-056-2

Although sendmail is used on almost every UNIX system, it's one of the last great uncharted territories—and most difficult utilities to learn—in UNIX system administration. This book provides a complete sendmail tutorial, plus extensive reference material. It covers the BSD, UIUC IDA, and V8 versions of sendmail.

"The program and its rule description file, sendmail.cf, have long been regarded as the pit of coals that separated the mild Unix system administrators from the real fire walkers. Now, sendmail syntax, testing, hidden rules, and other mysteries are revealed. Costales, Allman, and Rickert are the indisputable authorities to do the text."
—Ben Smith, *Byte*

Learning the UNIX Operating System

By Grace Todino, John Strang & Jerry Peek
3rd Edition August 1993
108 pages, ISBN 1-56592-060-0

If you are new to UNIX, this concise introduction will tell you just what you need to get started and no more. Why wade through a 600-page book when you can begin working productively in a matter of minutes? It's an ideal primer for Mac and PC users of the Internet who need to know a little bit about UNIX on the systems they visit. This book is the most effective introduction to UNIX in print. The third edition has been updated and expanded to provide increased coverage of window systems and networking. It's a handy book for someone just starting with UNIX, as well as someone who encounters a UNIX system as a "visitor" via remote login over the Internet.

Smileys

By David W. Sanderson
1st Edition March 1993
93 pages, ISBN 1-56592-041-4

From the people who put an armadillo on the cover of a system administrator book comes this collection of the computer underground hieroglyphs called "smileys." Originally inserted into email messages to denote "said with a cynical smile" :-), smileys now run rampant throughout the electronic mail culture.

!%@:: A Directory of Electronic Mail Addressing & Networks

By Donnalyn Frey & Rick Adams
4th Edition June 1994
662 pages, ISBN 1-56592-046-5

This is the only up-to-date directory that charts the networks that make up the Internet, provides contact names and addresses, and describes the services each network provides. It includes all of the major Internet-based networks, as well as various commercial networks such as CompuServe, Delphi, and America Online that are "gatewayed" to the Internet for transfer of electronic mail and other services. If you want to connect to the Internet or are already connected but want concise, up-to-date information on many of the world's networks, check out this book.

PGP: Pretty Good Privacy

By Simson Garfinkel
1st Edition December 1994
430 pages, ISBN 1-56592-098-8

PGP is a freely available encryption program that protects the privacy of files and electronic mail. It uses powerful public key cryptography and works on virtually every platform. This book is both a readable technical user's guide and a fascinating behind-the-scenes look at cryptography and privacy. It describes how to use PGP and provides background on cryptography, PGP's history, battles over public key cryptography patents and U.S. government export restrictions, and public debates about privacy and free speech.

"I even learned a few things about PGP from Simson's informative book."—Phil Zimmermann, Author of PGP

"Since the release of PGP 2.0 from Europe in the fall of 1992, PGP's popularity and usage has grown to make it the de-facto standard for email encryption. Simson's book is an excellent overview of PGP and the history of cryptography in general. It should prove a useful addition to the resource library for any computer user, from the UNIX wizard to the PC novice."
—Derek Atkins, PGP Development Team, MIT

Practical UNIX Security

By Simson Garfinkel & Gene Spafford
1st Edition June 1991
512 pages, ISBN 0-937175-72-2

Practical UNIX Security tells system administrators how to make their UNIX system—either System V or BSD—as secure as it possibly can be without going to trusted system technology. The book describes UNIX concepts and how they enforce security, tells how to defend against and handle security breaches, and explains network security (including UUCP, NFS, Kerberos, and firewall machines) in detail. If you are a UNIX system administrator or user who deals with security, you need this book.

"Timely, accurate, written by recognized experts...covers every imaginable topic relating to Unix security. An excellent book and I recommend it as a valuable addition to any system administrator's or computer site manager's collection."
—Jon Wright, *Informatics* (Australia)

Building Internet Firewalls

By D. Brent Chapman & Elizabeth D. Zwicky
1st Edition September 1995 (est.)
450 pages (est.), ISBN 1-56592-124-0

Everyone is jumping on the Internet bandwagon, despite the fact that the security risks associated with connecting to the Net have never been greater. This book is a practical guide to building firewalls on the Internet. It describes a variety of firewall approaches and architectures, and the details of how you can build packet filtering and proxying solutions at your site. It also contains a full discussion of how to configure Internet services (e.g., FTP, SMTP, Telnet) to work with a firewall, as well as a complete list of resources, including the location of many publicly available firewall construction tools.

Linux Network Administrator's Guide

By Olaf Kirch
1st Edition January 1995
370 pages, ISBN 1-56592-087-2

Linux, a UNIX-compatible operating system that runs on personal computers, is a pinnacle within the free software movement. It is based on a kernel developed by Finnish student Linus Torvalds and is distributed on the Net or on low-cost disks, along with a complete set of UNIX libraries, popular free software utilities, and traditional layered products like NFS and the X Window System.

Networking is a fundamental part of Linux. Whether you want a simple UUCP connection or a full LAN with NFS and NIS, you are going to have to build a network.

Linux Network Administrator's Guide by Olaf Kirch is one of the most successful books to come from the Linux Documentation Project. It touches on all the essential networking software included with Linux, plus some hardware considerations. Topics include serial connections, UUCP, routing and DNS, mail and News, SLIP and PPP, NFS, and NIS.

DNS and BIND

By Cricket Liu & Paul Albitz
1st Edition October 1992
418 pages, ISBN 1-56592-010-4

DNS and BIND contains all you need to know about the Internet's Domain Name System (DNS) and the Berkeley Internet Name Domain (BIND), its UNIX implementation. The Domain Name System is the Internet's "phone book"; it's a database that tracks important information (in particular, names and addresses) for every computer on the Internet. If you're a system administrator, this book will show you how to set up and maintain the DNS software on your network.

"At 418 pages it blows away easily any vendor supplied information, and because it has an extensive troubleshooting section (using nslookup) it should never be far from your desk—especially when things on your network start to go awry :-)"
—Ian Hoyle, BHP Research, Melbourne Laboratories

Learning Perl

By Randal L. Schwartz, Foreword by Larry Wall
1st Edition November 1993
274 pages, ISBN 1-56592-042-2

Learning Perl is ideal for system administrators, programmers, and anyone else wanting a down-to-earth introduction to this useful language. Written by a Perl trainer, its aim is to make a competent, hands-on Perl programmer out of the reader as quickly as possible. The book takes a tutorial approach and includes hundreds of short code examples, along with some lengthy ones. The relatively inexperienced programmer will find *Learning Perl* easily accessible.

Each chapter of the book includes practical programming exercises. Solutions are presented for all exercises.

For a comprehensive and detailed guide to advanced programming with Perl, read O'Reilly's companion book, *Programming perl*.

The Computer User's Survival Guide

By Joan Stigliani
1st Edition September 1995 (est.)
260 pages (est.), ISBN 1-56592-030-9

The bad news: You can be hurt by working at a computer. The good news: Many of the factors that pose a risk are within your control.

The Computer User's Survival Guide looks squarely at all the factors that affect your health on the job, including positioning, equipment, work habits, lighting, stress, radiation, and general health. It is not a book of gloom and doom. It is a guide to protecting yourself against health risks from your computer, while boosting your effectiveness and making your work more enjoyable.

This guide will teach you what's going on "under the skin" when your hands and arms spend much of the day mousing and typing and what you can do to prevent overuse injuries. You'll learn various postures to help reduce stress; what you can do to prevent glare from modern office lighting; simple breathing techniques and stretches to keep your body well oxygenated and relaxed; and how to reduce eye strain. Also covers radiation issues and what electrical equipment is responsible for the most exposure.

The Future Does Not Compute

By Stephen L. Talbott
1st Edition May 1995
502 pages, ISBN 1-56592-085-6

This book explores the networked computer as an expression of the darker, dimly conscious side of the human being. What we have been imparting to the Net—or what the Net has been eliciting from us—is a half-submerged, barely intended logic, contaminated by wishes and tendencies we prefer not to acknowledge. The urgent necessity is for us to wake up to what is most fully human and unmachinelike in ourselves, rather than yield to an ever more strangling embrace with our machines. The author's thesis is sure to raise a controversy among the millions of users now adapting themselves to the Net.

O'Reilly & Associates—
GLOBAL NETWORK NAVIGATOR™

The Global Network Navigator (GNN)™ is a unique kind of information service that makes the Internet easy and enjoyable to use. We organize access to the vast information resources of the Internet so that you can find what you want. We also help you understand the Internet and the many ways you can explore it.

What you'll find in GNN

There are three main sections to GNN: Navigating the Net, Special GNN Publications, and Marketplace.
Here's a look at just some of what's contained in GNN:

Navigating the Net

- The **WHOLE INTERNET USER'S GUIDE & CATALOG**, based on O'Reilly's bestselling book, is a collection of constantly updated links to 1000 of the best resources on the Internet, divided by subject areas.

- The **NCSA MOSAIC "WHAT'S NEW"** page is your best source for the latest Web listings. Browse it like you would a newspaper, then click on the new sites you're most interested in.

Special GNN Publications

- **BOOK STORY**—The first Internet platform to provide an interactive forum for authors and readers to meet. Serializes books, features author interviews and chats, and allows readers to contact authors with the ease of email.

- **TRAVELERS' CENTER**—The center takes advantage of information that's been on the Internet but hasn't been distilled and compiled in an easy-to-use format—until now. You'll also read feature stories and dispatches from fellow travelers.

- **PERSONAL FINANCE CENTER**—The money management and investment forum on the Net. There are original features and columns on personal finance, too.

- **GNN SPORTS**—Net coverage of your favorite professional and college teams with interviews, schedules, and game wrap-ups.

- **EDUCATION**—Tapping into the vast educational resources available on the Net.

- **NETNEWS**—Keep up with events, trends, and developments on the Net.

- **THE DIGITAL DRIVE-IN**—Read this GNN special edition to find out what folks are doing with multi-media resources on the Net.

Marketplace

- **BUSINESS PAGES**—Here's where we've organized commercial resources on the Internet. Choose from a variety of categories like "Business Services," "Entertainment," and "Legal Financial Services."

- **GNN DIRECT**—This is the place to go to read about quality products and services in GNN's collection of catalogs. You can also order online using GNN Direct. Simply browse through product literature, do key word and text searches, and place an order at any time.

Marketing Your Company on GNN

GNN is known as the premier interactive magazine and navigational guide on the Internet. With over 170,000 total subscribers and 8 million document hits every month, GNN attracts a large, dynamic, and growing audience. Because of this, GNN offers exciting opportunities for companies interested in creating a presence on the Internet. We currently offer two programs:

- **TRAFFIC LINKS**—We can link reader traffic from GNN to your Web site. Think of this option as an online form of direct response advertising. GNN staff will work with you to tailor a program to fit your needs. For details about this program, send email to **traffic-links@gnn.com** or call 1-510-883-7220 and ask for our Traffic Link sales representative.

- **BUSINESS PAGES**—Choose from a basic listing (up to 50 words), extended listing (up to 350 words), links from your listing in GNN to your server, or a FAQ (Frequently Asked Questions) document of up to 350 words that's coupled with either a basic or extended listing. For more information, send email to **market@gnn.com** or call 1-510-883-7220.

Get Your Free Subscription to GNN Today

Come and browse GNN! A free subscription is available to anyone with access to the World Wide Web. To get complete information about subscribing, send email to **info@gnn.com**

If you have access to a World Wide Web browser such as Mosaic, Lynx, or NetScape, use the following URL to register online:
`http://gnn.com/`

If you use a browser that does not support online forms, you can retrieve an email version of the registration form automatically by sending email to **form@gnn.com** Fill this form out and send it back to us by email and we will confirm your registration.

AUDIOTAPES

O'Reilly now offers audiotapes based on interviews with people who are making a profound impact in the world of the Internet. Here we give you a quick overview of what's available. For details on our audiotape collection, send email to **audio@ora.com**.

"Ever listen to one of those five-minute-long news pieces being broadcast on National Public Radio's 'All Things Considered' and wish they were doing an in-depth story on new technology? Well, your wishes are answered." —Byte

Global Network Operations

Carl Malamud interviews Brian Carpenter, Bernhard Stockman, Mike O'Dell, & Geoff Huston
Duration: 2 hours, ISBN 1-56592-993-4

What does it take to actually run a network? In these four interviews, Carl Malamud explores some of the technical and operational issues faced by Internet service providers around the world.

Brian Carpenter is the director for networking at CERN, the high-energy physics laboratory in Geneva, Switzerland. Physicists are some of the world's most active Internet users, and its global user base makes CERN one of the world's most network-intensive sites. Carpenter discusses how he deals with issues such as the OSI and DECnet Phase V protocols and his views on the future of the Internet.

Bernhard Stockman is one of the founders and the technical manager of the European Backbone (EBONE). EBONE has proven to be the first effective transit backbone for Europe and has been a leader in the deployment of CIDR, BGP-4, and other key technologies.

Mike O'Dell is vice president of research at UUNET Technologies. O'Dell has a long record of involvement in data communications, ranging from his service as a telco lab employee, an engineer on several key projects, and a member of the USENIX board, to now helping define new services for one of the largest commercial IP service providers.

Geoff Huston is the director of the Australian Academic Research Network (AARNET). AARNET is known as one of the most progressive regional networks, rapidly adopting new services for its users. Huston talks about how networking in Australia has flourished despite astronomically high rates for long-distance lines.

The Future of the Internet Protocol

Carl Malamud interviews Steve Deering, Bob Braden, Christian Huitema, Bob Hinden, Peter Ford, Steve Casner, Bernhard Stockman, & Noel Chiappa
Duration: 4 hours, ISBN 1-56592-996-9

The explosion of interest in the Internet is stressing what was originally designed as a research and education network. The sheer number of users is requiring new strategies for Internet address allocation; multimedia applications are requiring greater bandwidth and strategies such as "resource reservation" to provide synchronous end-to-end service.

In this series of eight interviews, Carl Malamud talks to some of the researchers who are working to define how the underlying technology of the Internet will need to evolve in order to meet the demands of the next five to ten years.

Give these tapes a try if you're intrigued by such topics as Internet "multicasting" of audio and video, or think your job might one day depend on understanding some of the following buzzwords:

- IPNG (Internet Protocol Next Generation)
- SIP (Simple Internet Protocol)
- TUBA (TCP and UDP with Big Addresses)
- CLNP (Connectionless Network Protocol)
- CIDR (Classless Inter-Domain Routing)

or if you are just interested in getting to know more about the people who are shaping the future.

Mobile IP Networking

Carl Malamud interviews Phil Karn & Jun Murai
Released September 1994
Duration: 1 hour, ISBN 1-56592-994-2

Phil Karn is the father of the KA9Q publicly-available implementation of TCP/IP for DOS (which has also been used as the basis for the software in many commercial Internet routers). KA9Q was originally developed to allow "packet radio," that is, TCP/IP over ham radio bands. Phil's current research focus is on commercial applications of wireless data communications.

Jun Murai is one of the most distinguished researchers in the Internet community. Murai is a professor at Keio University and the founder of the Japanese WIDE Internet. Murai talks about his research projects, which range from satellite-based IP multicasting to a massive testbed for mobile computing at the Fujisawa campus of Keio University.

Networked Information and Online Libraries

Carl Malamud interviews Peter Deutsch & Cliff Lynch
Released September 1993
Duration: 1 hour, ISBN 1-56592-998-5

Peter Deutsch, president of Bunyip Information Services, was one of the co-developers of Archie. In this interview Peter talks about his philosophy for services and compares Archie to X.500. He also talks about what kind of standards we need for networked information retrieval.

Cliff Lynch is currently the director of library automation for the University of California. He discusses issues behind online publishing, such as SGML and the democratization of publishing on the Internet.

European Networking

Carl Malamud interviews Glenn Kowack & Rob Blokzijl
Released September 1993
Duration: 1 hour, ISBN 1-56592-999-3

Glenn Kowack is chief executive of EUnet, the network that's bringing the Internet to the people of Europe. Glenn talks about EUnet's populist business model and the politics of European networking.

Rob Blokzijl is the network manager for NIKHEF, the Dutch Institute of High Energy Physics. Rob talks about RIPE, the IP user's group for Europe, and the nuts and bolts of European network coordination.

Security and Networks

Carl Malamud interviews Jeff Schiller & John Romkey
Released September 1993
Duration: 1 hour, ISBN 1-56592-997-7

Jeff Schiller is the manager of MIT's campus network and is one of the Internet's leading security experts. Here, he talks about Privacy Enhanced Mail (PEM), the difficulty of policing the Internet, and whether horses or computers are more useful to criminals.

John Romkey has been a long-time TCP/IP developer and was recently named to the Internet Architecture Board. In this wide-ranging interview, John talks about the famous "ToasterNet" demo at InterOp, what kind of Internet security he'd like to see put in place, and what Internet applications of the future might look like.

John Perry Barlow
Notable Speeches of the Information Age

USENIX Conference Keynote Address
San Francisco, CA; January 17, 1994
Duration: 1.5 hours, ISBN 1-56592-992-6

John Perry Barlow—retired Wyoming cattle rancher, lyricist for the Grateful Dead—holds a degree in comparative religion from Wesleyan University. He also happens to be a recognized authority on computer security, virtual reality, digitized intellectual property, and the social and legal conditions arising in the global network of computers.

In 1990, Barlow co-founded the Electronic Frontier Foundation with Mitch Kapor and currently serves as chair of its executive committee. He writes and lectures on subjects relating to digital technology and society, and is a contributing editor to *Communications of the ACM*, *NeXTWorld*, *Microtimes*, *Mondo 2000*, *Wired*, and other publications.

In his keynote address to the Winter 1994 USENIX Conference, Barlow talks of recent developments in the national information infrastructure, telecommunications regulation, cryptography, globalization of the Internet, intellectual property, and the settlement of Cyberspace. The talk explores the premise that "architecture is politics": that the technology adopted for the coming "information superhighway" will help to determine what is carried on it and that if the electronic frontier of the Internet is not to be replaced by electronic strip malls, we need to make sure that our technological choices favor bi-directional communication and open platforms.

Side A contains the keynote;
Side B contains a question and answer period.

O'Reilly on the Net—
ONLINE PROGRAM GUIDE

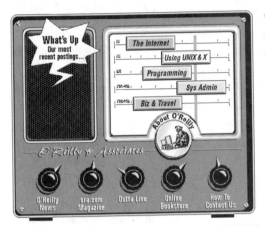

O'Reilly & Associates offers extensive information through various online resources. We invite you to come and explore our little neck-of-the-woods.

Online Resource Center

Most comprehensive among our online offerings is the O'Reilly Resource Center. Here, you'll find detailed information on all O'Reilly products: titles, prices, tables of contents, indexes, author bios, software contents, reviews...you can even view images of the products themselves. With GNN Direct you can now order our products directly off the Net (GNN Direct is available on the Web site only; Gopher users can still use **order@ora.com**). We supply contact information along with a list of distributors and bookstores available worldwide. In addition, we provide informative literature in the field: articles, interviews, excerpts, and bibliographies that help you stay informed and abreast.

To access ORA's Online Resource Center:

Point your Web browser (e.g., **mosaic** or **lynx**) to:

`http://www.ora.com/`

For the plaintext version, **telnet** or **gopher** to:

`gopher.ora.com`

(telnet login: **gopher**)

FTP

The example files and programs in many of our books are available electronically via FTP.

To obtain example files and programs from O'Reilly texts:

`ftp` to:

`ftp.ora.com`

or `ftp.uu.net`
`cd published/oreilly`

Ora-news

An easy way to stay informed of the latest projects and products from O'Reilly & Associates is to subscribe to "ora-news," our electronic news service. Subscribers receive email as soon as the information breaks.

To subscribe to "ora-news":

Send email to:
listproc@online.ora.com

and put the following information on the first line of your message (not in "Subject"):
subscribe ora-news "your name" **of** "your company"

For example enter:

`mail listproc@online.ora.com`

`subscribe ora-news Kris Webber of`
`    Mighty Fine Enterprises`

Email

Many customer services are provided via email. Here are a few of the most popular and useful.

nuts@ora.com
> For general questions and information.

bookquestions@ora.com
> For technical questions, or corrections, concerning book contents.

order@ora.com
> To order books online and for ordering questions.

catalog@online.ora.com
> To receive a free copy of our magazine/catalog, *ora.com*. Please include a postal address.

Snailmail and Phones

O'Reilly & Associates, Inc.
103A Morris Street, Sebastopol, CA 95472
Inquiries: **707-829-0515, 800-998-9938**
Credit card orders: **800-889-8969** (Weekdays 6 A.M.- 5 P.M. PST)
FAX: 707-829-0104

O'Reilly & Associates—
LISTING OF TITLES

INTERNET

!%@:: A Directory of Electronic Mail
  Addressing & Networks
Connecting to the Internet:
  An O'Reilly Buyer's Guide
The Mosaic Handbook for
  Microsoft Windows
The Mosaic Handbook for
  the Macintosh
The Mosaic Handbook for
  the X Window System
Smileys
The Whole Internet User's
  Guide & Catalog

SOFTWARE

Internet In A Box™
WebSite™

WHAT YOU NEED TO KNOW SERIES

Using Email Effectively
Marketing on the Internet
  (Fall '95 est.)
When You Can't Find Your
  System Administrator

HEALTH, CAREER & BUSINESS

Building a Successful Software Business
The Computer User's Survival Guide
  (Fall '95 est.)
The Future Does Not Compute
Love Your Job!
TWI Day Calendar - 1996

AUDIOTAPES

INTERNET TALK RADIO'S "GEEK OF THE WEEK" INTERVIEWS

The Future of the Internet Protocol
Global Network Operations
Mobile IP Networking
Networked Information and
  Online Libraries
Security and Networks
European Networking

NOTABLE SPEECHES OF THE INFORMATION AGE

John Perry Barlow

USING UNIX

BASICS

Learning GNU Emacs
Learning the Korn Shell
Learning the UNIX Operating System
Learning the vi Editor
MH & xmh: Email for Users &
  Programmers
SCO UNIX in a Nutshell
The USENET Handbook
Using UUCP and Usenet
UNIX in a Nutshell: System V Edition

ADVANCED

Exploring Expect
The Frame Handbook
Learning Perl
Making TeX Work
Programming perl
Running LINUX
sed & awk
UNIX Power Tools (with CD-ROM)

SYSTEM ADMINISTRATION

Building Internet Firewalls
  (Fall '95 est.)
Computer Crime: A Crimefighter's
  Handbook (Summer '95 est.)
Computer Security Basics
DNS and BIND
Essential System Administration
Linux Network Administrator's Guide
Managing Internet Information Services
Managing NFS and NIS
Managing UUCP and Usenet
Networking Personal Computers
  with TCP/IP (Summer '95 est.)
Practical UNIX Security
PGP: Pretty Good Privacy
sendmail
System Performance Tuning
TCP/IP Network Administration
termcap & terminfo
Volume 8 : X Window System
  Administrator's Guide
The X Companion CD for R6

PROGRAMMING

Applying RCS and SCCS
  (Summer '95 est.)
Checking C Programs with lint
DCE Security Programming
  (Summer '95 est.)
Distributing Applications Across DCE
  and Windows NT
Encyclopedia of Graphics File Formats
Guide to Writing DCE Applications
High Performance Computing
Learning the Bash Shell (Summer '95
  est.)
lex & yacc
Managing Projects with make
Microsoft RPC Programming Guide
Migrating to Fortran 90
Multi-Platform Code Management
ORACLE Performance Tuning
ORACLE PL/SQL Programming
  (Fall '95 est.)
Porting UNIX Software (Fall '95 est.)
POSIX Programmer's Guide
POSIX.4: Programming for
  the Real World
Power Programming with RPC
Practical C Programming
Practical C++ Programming
  (Summer '95 est.)
Programming with curses
Programming with GNU Software
  (Fall '95 est.)
Software Portability with imake
Understanding and Using COFF
Understanding DCE
Understanding Japanese Information
  Processing
UNIX for FORTRAN Programmers
Using C on the UNIX System
Using csh and tcsh (Summer '95 est.)

BERKELEY 4.4 SOFTWARE DISTRIBUTION

4.4BSD System Manager's Manual
4.4BSD User's Reference Manual
4.4BSD User's Supplementary
  Documents
4.4BSD Programmer's Reference
  Manual
4.4BSD Programmer's Supplementary
  Documents
4.4BSD-Lite CD Companion
4.4BSD-Lite CD Companion:
  International Version

X PROGRAMMING

THE X WINDOW SYSTEM

Volume 0: X Protocol Reference Manual
Volume 1: Xlib Programming Manual
Volume 2: Xlib Reference Manual:
Volume 3: X Window System
  User's Guide
Volume. 3M: X Window System
  User's Guide, Motif Ed.
Volume. 4: X Toolkit Intrinsics
  Programming Manual
Volume 4M: X Toolkit Intrinsics
  Programming Manual, Motif Ed.
Volume 5: X Toolkit Intrinsics
  Reference Manual
Volume 6A: Motif Programming
  Manual
Volume 6B: Motif Reference Manual
Volume 7A: XView Programming
  Manual
Volume 7B: XView Reference Manual
Volume 8 : X Window System
  Administrator's Guide
PEXlib Programming Manual
PEXlib Reference Manual
PHIGS Programming Manual
PHIGS Reference Manual
Programmer's Supplement for Release 6
  (Fall '95 est.)
Motif Tools (with CD-ROM)
The X Companion CD for R6
The X Window System in a Nutshell
X User Tools (with CD-ROM)

THE X RESOURCE

A QUARTERLY WORKING JOURNAL FOR X PROGRAMMERS

The X Resource: Issues 0 through 15
  (Issue 15 available 7/95)

TRAVEL

Travelers' Tales France
Travelers' Tales Hong Kong (10/95 est.)
Travelers' Tales India
Travelers' Tales Mexico
Travelers' Tales Spain (11/95 est.)
Travelers' Tales Thailand
Travelers' Tales: A Woman's World

O'Reilly & Associates—
INTERNATIONAL DISTRIBUTORS

Customers outside North America can now order O'Reilly & Associates books through the following distributors. They offer our international customers faster order processing, more bookstores, increased representation at tradeshows worldwide, and the high-quality, responsive service our customers have come to expect.

EUROPE, MIDDLE EAST, AND AFRICA
(except Germany, Switzerland, and Austria)

INQUIRIES
International Thomson Publishing Europe
Berkshire House
168-173 High Holborn
London WC1V 7AA, United Kingdom
Telephone: 44-71-497-1422
Fax: 44-71-497-1426
Email: itpint@itps.co.uk

ORDERS
International Thomson Publishing Services, Ltd.
Cheriton House, North Way
Andover, Hampshire SP10 5BE, United Kingdom
Telephone: 44-264-342-832 (UK orders)
Telephone: 44-264-342-806 (outside UK)
Fax: 44-264-364418 (UK orders)
Fax: 44-264-342761 (outside UK)

GERMANY, SWITZERLAND, AND AUSTRIA

International Thomson Publishing GmbH
O'Reilly-International Thomson Verlag
Königswinterer Straße 418
53227 Bonn, Germany
Telephone: 49-228-97024 0
Fax: 49-228-441342
Email: anfragen@ora.de

ASIA *(except Japan)*
INQUIRIES
International Thomson Publishing Asia
221 Henderson Road
#08-03 Henderson Industrial Park
Singapore 0315
Telephone: 65-272-6496
Fax: 65-272-6498

ORDERS
Telephone: 65-268-7867
Fax: 65-268-6727

JAPAN
International Thomson Publishing Japan
Hirakawa-cho Kyowa Building 3F
2-2-1 Hirakawa-cho, Chiyoda-Ku
Tokyo, 102 Japan
Telephone: 81-3-3221-1428
Fax: 81-3-3237-1459

Toppan Publishing
Froebel Kan Bldg. 3-1, Kanda Ogawamachi Chiyoda-Ku
Tokyo 101 Japan
Telex: J 27317
Cable: Toppanbook, Tokyo
Telephone: 03-3295-3461
Fax: 03-3293-5963

AUSTRALIA
WoodsLane Pty. Ltd.
7/5 Vuko Place, Warriewood NSW 2102
P.O. Box 935, Mona Vale NSW 2103
Australia
Telephone: 02-970-5111
Fax: 02-970-5002
Email: woods@tmx.mhs.oz.au

NEW ZEALAND
WoodsLane New Zealand Ltd.
21 Cooks Street (P.O. Box 575)
Wanganui, New Zealand
Telephone: 64-6-347-6543
Fax: 64-6-345-4840
Email: woods@tmx.mhs.oz.au

THE AMERICAS
O'Reilly & Associates, Inc.
103A Morris Street
Sebastopol, CA 95472 U.S.A.
Telephone: 707-829-0515
Telephone: 800-998-9938 (U.S. & Canada)
Fax: 707-829-0104
Email: order@ora.com